V. Papadin (signature)

TEACH YOURSELF
TO BE A MADMAN

MEMORIES OF A YOUNG RUSSIAN SOLDIER

D1557148

Illustrated by the author
Valentin Papadin
1993

Published by
Burning Bush Publishing
283 Sherwood Road
Willits, CA 95490

PRINTED IN THE UNITED STATES OF AMERICA

TEACH YOURSELF TO BE

A Madman

MEMORIES OF A YOUNG RUSSIAN SOLDIER

Dedicated to my invisible guardian angels.

INTRODUCTION

It is the glory of some men to write well, and of others not to write at all.
La Bruyere

Men are so necessarily mad that not to be mad would amount to another form of madness.
Pascal

This book is recommended for:
INMATES ON DEATH ROW
PACIFISTS IN COUNTRIES WITH COMPULSORY
MILITARY SERVICE

My dear friends, I hope you have not jumped to the wrong conclusion, that I am some kind of expert, a Ph.D. in medical science.

No, No, I am not a fat psychiatrist with a twitching eye and the obscure Latin of a Catholic mass. On the contrary, I am one who fought many doctors for many weeks in a private, secret war, by faking madness.

For me it was the only way to get out of the Soviet Army.

I didn't want to be a soldier, especially in Russia. Maybe on the island of New Guinea, among Papuans, I would not mind being a warrior, shooting at lions with poisonous arrows, but in my Motherland every training target has a man's silhouette, a profile of someone's life.

For me, whether to kill or be killed was equally sickening. In both cases the stink of death clouded my imagination.

It was not that I decided to get a discharge, it was simply a deep feeling of certainty that nothing in the world could possibly force me to do what I didn't want to do even if I had to go to court martial.

I was 18 - the age when a compromise with your own conscience scares you more than the iron gates of prison.

God and ignorance made me brave.

Part I

FIT TO BE DEAD

CHAPTER 1

Can anything be more ridiculous than that a man should have the right to kill me because he lives on the other side of the water, and because his ruler has a quarrel with mine?

Pascal

AND NOW, AS IN ANY "TEACH YOURSELF BOOK", I'll let my experience revolve around drawings.

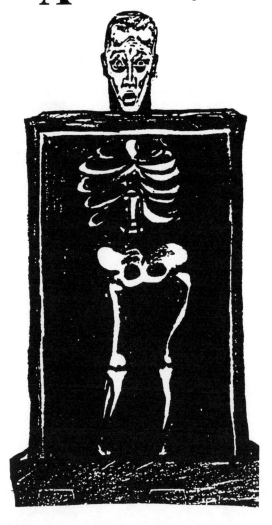

"Conscript Papadin, you are fit to serve in any branch of our glorious Armed Forces. Soon the peaceful sleep of our children and the whole planet will be your personal responsibility. Congratulations!"

The chairman of the Conscript Medical Examination Committee, a very old toothless man, shook my hand and soaked the right sleeve of my shirt with his dripping saliva-- his bottom lip leaking like the door of a defrosting fridge. I gave him a polite smile (I didn't like to be rude to seniors even when I thought their views to be just a reprint of newspapers).

Apart from bringing me the bad news about my good health, the Examination was a positive event because from that very morning I started thinking seriously about going crazy. The idea came to me while being examined:

A therapist checked my blood pressure, the pressure of life.

A surgeon poked at my brains through my ear holes with a tiny flashlight.

A dermatologist, looking for signs of sexual diseases, used our own fingers to check our private parts and to peel back our foreskins - red illusion of circumcision.

The radiologist, like a magician behind his black box, nuked our lungs with X-rays.

This was the observation I made:

All the specialists, to make a diagnosis, needed PHYSICAL contact with PHYSICAL BODIES, they hardly talked to us, they didn't have to. And only the female psychiatrist relied on words, on dialogs, on my answers. I realized she could be influenced right there, on the spot, and therefore her conclusions about my mental state would change accordingly !!!!!!!!!!!!!!!!!!!!!!!!!!!!!!!!! Terrific! What a potential! Viva the foggy spiritual world where nobody can see clearly! Of course, that morning I didn't push my luck. I didn't mumble schizophrenic nonsense. I was not ready.

Plus:

The authorities were simply ready to expect a bunch of tricks from conscripts. It's traditional. Until we became proper soldiers, enslaved by the patriotic military oath and guilt towards our Motherland, we were all under the magnifying glass of suspicion. Any fooling around at this stage would have been profoundly stupid.

Plus:

The psychiatrist was such a pretty Latvian blond that at her standard professional question "Do you ever wet the bed?" I could not possibly say a sneaky "yes". Not that time. Even for the sake of a discharge. I was a poet, a poet from 7th grade to eternity. It meant I was predisposed to the influence of women's beauty and eclipses of the moon.

After the Examination, on the way home, I whispered to the autumn sky: "If God really loves me, my next psychiatrist will either be a man or a very ugly woman with non-stop hiccups".

Chapter 2

Fortune turns everything to the advantage of those she favors.
Francois, Duke de La Rochefoucauld

T WO WEEKS LATER (OCTOBER 3RD) ON A REGULAR visit to the City Military Committee I was told the number of my team - 37- a code, which stood for the famous nuclear submarine 'Chelyabinsky Komsomolets'. This news devastated me.

First of all, I doubted that the squashed labyrinths of a submarine would provide enough light, space and audience for my performance as a madman.

Second, if I ever chickened out and stopped being crazy as a fox I would be faced with full service in the Navy which lasts a year longer than the ground Forces, three instead of two.

Third, I didn't like the source of power 'Komsomolets' used. I had heard rumors about disastrous effects of nuclear reactors on the most intimate activity of crew members.

Finally, like anything welded in the Soviet Union the submarine would not have been much stronger than a barrel for pickled cucumbers.

Well, well, well, I got in a panic. I was trapped by the speed with which bad events were approaching me.

'What's the quickest way to get out of this mess? Chop off the fingers on my right hand? Or maybe jump from the second floor, breaking one of my legs if not two? Brrrrrrrrrrrrrrr, yukkky! No, no, no. Why should I cripple myself? It's never too late for masochism. I can go to extremes when nothing else is left. Let's wait and see. I much prefer to use my intelligence instead of an ax.'

I found a specific goal - to become a strange depressing zombie, like my poor friend and classmate Vaska Ryabuhin. He was hospitalized and diagnosed 'schizophrenic - paranoid form' just before graduation from High School. He would be the perfect one to copy.

I remember well how the illness gradually transformed a nice clever boy into an annoying misanthrope, our friendship into a nightmare. Vaska had schizophrenia running in the family. He inherited defective genes from his mother. Such nasty genes, like the seeds of weeds, sprout in the most humid season - when you are a teenager.

It took Vaska approximately a year to go totally nuts. I would have to do it faster.

Sometimes I thought: should I not openly, in public, burn my military ticket? On the one hand it would be a rare heroic gesture. On the other hand what would I achieve? A sentence to labor camp for 4 years and passionate attention from prison mates who interpret the Lord's command 'Love One Another' too literally.

No. I'm an old fashioned boy.

October 10th brought sweet encouragement. The team number was changed to #15, the Air Force. Good, very good. I hate the Navy. I much prefer a falling airplane to a sinking boat - the agony is shorter.

At home, on the wall-calendar, I circled the departure date - October 18. I had precisely seven days to say good-by to all my relatives and seven nights for intensive seduction of my girlfriend Luba.

Because of her conservative morals both of us stayed virgins. She used to say when we hugged 'You can kiss me..the rest is after the wedding'.

'What cruel stubbornness. What if I never come back from the army, get shot, eh? Eh? What will she do with all that trembling cobweb over her purity, eh?

Honestly, it does not make any sense. She thinks if I write poems every evening that I can constantly live on the clouds. She is badly mistaken. I also want meat in my menu. And I myself am beefy. Inspiration comes and goes but rattling in the balls after a juicy kiss lasts forever and I have to live with it.'

CHAPTER 3

All women look pretty from a distance, in the dusk under a paper umbrella.
Japanese Proverb

"WRITE TO US. SEND US YOUR NEW ADDRESS as soon as you know."
The nagging of my relatives in the backyard of the Military
Commissariat deepened my worries caused by the uncertainty as to
where exactly I would serve. Soviet air bases are all over the world, starting
from the Ural Mountains, to the lazy island of Cuba and the Kuril Islands
grabbed from Japan in 1945.

The officer in charge of our team lined us up (about 40 guys) and checked every rucksack for alcohol and playing cards. He kept refusing even to hint where he was taking us. Only once he winked sarcastically: "Where? To the train." It was true. We rode to the railway station on two big army trucks. Tears from the wind and grief made me shortsighted.

For several minutes Luba followed our truck with her cousin in his beaten up 'Moscvich'. She was waving, sending air kisses, but I didn't respond much. I didn't feel sexy at all. Fear of the future castrated me.

The condition of the old steam engine and worn out pre-war wagons suggested that we weren't going to travel very far and that our military base was somewhere near. Wishful thinking. Russia again proved to be a country of possible impossibilities. On that train we covered a distance of more than 3,000 miles, from Western Siberia to the Far East, in 12 days. In Chelyabinsk, on the second day of the journey, extra weight was added - about a thousand other conscripts - the main chunk of team #15.

Riding that train helped me to learn more about my capacity to withstand cold, hunger, filth and stiff boredom.

We were crossing Siberia from left to right, moving from autumn to winter. For some mysterious reason no blankets were given. Only mattresses, dirty and stripy, like corpses of war prisoners. You woke up at night from your own coughing and couldn't get back to sleep because of someone else's.

Our empty stomachs doubled the effect of the cold. Even at long stops in big cities we were not allowed to leave the trucks and buy food at the station buffets to supplement the disgusting glue-like gruel given twice a day. But even more indigestible were the hours of daily 'political information'. Two sergeants, in turns, would walk through the compartments explaining to us why the Soviet People are the happiest in the world. As a rule their Ukrainian accent was mixed with a strong odor of alcohol, onions and aftershave - a combination typical of the lowest commanding level. The officers that passed through had a more expensive burp of chocolate and cognac.

None of them ever noticed the illegal passenger, a 12 year old boy, dressed in a cute sailor's suit, who had been hiding under the first tier of the wooden bunk and riding with us for many days. All I knew about the boy was that his name was Alyosha, that he was probably a younger brother of one of the conscripts and had sneaked on the train through the window, somewhere near Sverdlovsck. Alyosha's presence on the train intensified my sarcasm towards the arrogant self-pleased officers who thought they had everything under control. Several times I tried to talk to Alyosha but he kept his distance with a polite smiling silence. He even refused to let me wipe away the blood from a fresh scratch on his forehead.

At night when all commanders were asleep or drunk each wagon would catch up with normal habitual life: spicy jokes, playing cards, fist fighting. For many reasons I was spending most of the time on the third tier. There I was closer to the warmish heating pipe near the ceiling and far from the restless troublemakers. There, invisible, I practiced different facial expressions to match with those of that precious psycho Vaska. I trained my eyes, cheeks and lips to recreate his arrogant mystic smile.

Gradually I moved my silent acting from the dark corners into the daylight. The result was totally unexpected: I was noticed, yes, but also immediately promoted. Sergeant Borzenko put me in charge of the compartment.

'Very upsetting promotion! What's going on? The stranger I look the more respected I become...' Then, remembering a proverb 'Everything is for the best', I realized the advantages of having the reputation of a zealous soldier: he would be the last one to be suspected of cheating. So later when I increased my craziness it would look like nothing but a genuine disease.

"Several times I tried to talk to Alyosha but he kept his distance with a polite smiling silence. He even refused to let me wipe away the blood from a fresh scratch on his forehead."

CHAPTER 4

Never having been able to succeed in the world, he took revenge by speaking ill of it.

Voltaire

OUR DESTINATION- SPASSK-DALNIY, A SMALL TOWN BORN by merging three villages. Ten miles from the Chinese border, one hundred from the Pacific Ocean. One story wooden houses. Narrow twisted streets. No pedestrians, no hope at all to meet a pretty girl.

How can people stay sane in such a place? A trap for youth's dreams. The dump of the universe.

It was difficult to breathe: -34° C with the humidity of a laundry room. We marched towards our military base. Our stretched column was outlined by the sergeants' swearing and the occasional giggling of civilian pedestrians. We looked a mess in our threadbare clothes. Our families had dressed us specially in rags which would be thrown out as soon as we were issued uniforms: no point in junking good clothes.

At the base, behind the closed gate with the welded red star, in front of the brick barracks, we were sorted into companies and platoons. Then, jumping from frost bite, we listened to our source of worldly wisdom - a tall colonel with a stiff gray mustache sticking up like bull's horns that were most probably the main factor behind his successful military career. If the colonel had been wearing my beret and dirty towel for a scarf instead of his warm cossack hat, his speech would have been much shorter.

This is a summary of his babbling: Four companies would study airplane engines, four others (including mine) would be trained as bomb mechanics. The situation in the world was tense. Chinese extremists, betraying the ideas of Marxism-Leninism, were getting more dangerous than Brits and Yankees. The future of the world depended on how well we studied in class.

In the gymnasium building we cut each other's hair with dull clippers, then in turns, by companies, went to the bathhouse - a basement which had once been a shooting range and now - only water pipes under the ceiling. Through perforations in the pipes water jetted down on us, first very cold, then very hot, then just rusty dripping. The slivers of household soap kept slipping like cockroaches through our fingers or getting stuck between embarrassed buttocks.

Looking around, summarizing all this roughness, dirt and indifference to us raw conscripts, sparked off my fear, that maybe the whole regiment was going to be sacrificed in the next clash on the Chinese border.

We were drunk with exhaustion. We fell asleep fast without joking around. As soon as my back touched the bed my head rolled down into the basket of darkness as if it had been guillotined by ghosts from the French Revolution.

CHAPTER 5

Patriotism is the last refuge of scoundrels.

G. K. Chesterton

PEOPLE SAY 'WHERE THE AIR FORCE STARTS order ends' but not in my platoon, is that clear? You two are going to keep everybody in line and behave yourselves, without jerking around, or I will nail your Siberian penises to broomsticks and have you sweep the floors. Good luck."

Sergeant Borzenko, obviously humbled by his hangover, was unusually laconic and soft-spoken the next morning. Also he must have been blinded by it. Otherwise he would not have made team leaders out of me and Borka Koverda. Borka was as determined as I was to get out of the army. Only he never hid his intentions, he didn't lead a double game like I did, he was openly trying to get an ulcer by drinking daily all kinds of diluted acids. But so far he still had his pink cheeks and sparkling eyes, like an exemplary soldier on the posters.

Initial military training took a bit over a month. It consisted mainly of heavy labor on building sites rather than marching and drilling. The end of training was marked by the most pompous ceremony in my life: taking the military oath.

On Sunday morning, after breakfast, we lined up in the barracks with our personal assault rifles - 7.62mm Kalashnikov rifles - across our chests. Patriotic music over the broadcast system made us feel tall, smart, immortal.

Live speech by the company commander. Then two soldiers and a sergeant with the popped eyes of a boiled fish marched impressively with the huge regiment banner from the glass toilet door to the center of the dormitory. Finally, a Tartar recruit, Usupka Kusimov, started reading loudly the text of the Oath, which we all repeated with macho roughness in our voices:

MILITARY OATH

I, Valentin Papadin, a citizen of the Soviet Socialist Republics, by joining the ranks of the armed forces, take an oath and solemnly swear to be an upright, brave, disciplined, vigilant soldier, to strictly preserve military and government secrets, and to carry out without contradiction, all military regulations and orders of commanders and superiors. I swear to conscientiously learn the trade of war, to protect by all means the military and people's property, and to be devoted to my people, my Soviet homeland, and the Soviet Government until my last breath. I will always be ready to report, by order of the Soviet Government, as a soldier of the armed forces for the defense of my homeland, the Union of Soviet Socialist Republics. I swear to defend it bravely and wisely with all my strength and blood and without regard for my life in order to achieve a total victory over the enemy. Should I break the solemn oath, may the severe penalties of the Soviet Law, the overall hatred, and the contempt of the working masses strike me.

Usupka was chosen for that important role in order to remind us and invisible capitalist spies that in the Soviet Union every nation is treated equally, that everybody, without partiality, can be made a prisoner or a soldier.

On November 22 we officially became defenders of our Motherland. A week later all team leaders, including me, by the written order of the regiment commander, were given the rank of corporal. With that came a red stripe across the shoulder-loop. And the stripe, like any sign of authority, sparked off envious grumbling.

There were 32 guys in our 1st platoon. Naturally some of them were more suitable than I to become a successful team leader - more popular, more muscular, more dumb. Such guys treated my promotion as a social injustice. But during basic training everyone had been absorbed by beginner's stress and only now did they begin to growl at the fact that I had what I didn't deserve - legal power over half of them. They didn't like it.

So they opposed me by ignoring or being sloppy in following my commands though my commands were just a paraphrase of the sergeant's or lieutenant's orders. After several cases of flunking jobs and bending the regulations, my team, including me, was put on the black list by our superiors which meant extra work and graveyard shift. Pretty soon, as a result of several night duties, added to the regular slavery, lack of sleep caught up with us, wore us out, chewed off the best in our characters and thickened the team's bitterness towards me. My steady arrogance, which stemmed from continuously impersonating a schizophrenic, eventually caused a crisis in relations:

It happened one day on the airfield, in the break between practical lessons of bomb lifting. Popov, Naumov, Hantel and Levchuk started pushing each other onto me, from behind, so that I couldn't tell exactly who the pusher was. I was going to tolerate that energetic foolishness until they almost knocked me down and Popov, instead of saying 'sorry' did the opposite - engraved my name in long dirty swearing which I didn't let him finish - I jumped at him, hit his jaw with a left swing, which stunned him, and then bombarded his face with heavy blows, hating myself for losing self-control and hating that green brainless mess called the Armed Forces. Thanks to Popov's bruised Soviet mug the platoon mates' respect for me was temporarily restored. But this time Sergeant Borzenko finally realized that there was a much bigger conflict behind that small incident, that I could be the direct cause of many misfortunes following the team. His enthusiasm towards me noticeably cooled. He didn't hurry to tell a fresh joke if I was nearby.

Then, a couple of days later, after my knuckles, disturbed in fighting, prevented me from scoring the minimum at the inter regiment shooting competition, Borzenko completely turned his back on me. Several times I spotted him and the lieutenant having confidential chats and looking in my direction with disapproving glances. I felt they might have been discussing the possibility of replacing me with someone else. Hard luck. It wouldn't be easy since I wasn't just a team leader but a corporal. A private can't take command over a corporal unless it's in combat action where the corporal is wounded and immobilized.

The attitude I had to my superiors was contradictory. In some way, as a still warm-blooded human being I felt sorry for them trapped with me, a promoted trouble-maker. On the other hand I had a pleasant revengeful tickling in my nostrils -'It serves you right, bastards. Stop thinking you know everything.'

CHAPTER 6

To live we need only a short life; to act we need a long one.

THE MORE PRESSURE THE ARMY WAS PUTTING ON me the more concentrated and thorough my imitation of Vaska Ryabuhin was becoming. Like deaf Beethoven leaning on the vibration of the piano I eagerly absorbed with all my body the memories about Vaska's sluggishness, listlessness, half-sleepiness.

I let my tongue and lips become like rubber in reproducing his slow, pseudo-clever phrases. To achieve an effect of deadly indifference to the whole world I trained my eyeballs to roll over roofs, horizons, military hats, avoiding such glassy stuff like people's eyes and barracks windows.

Day after day, week after week passed ...nobody paid any attention to me... Obviously there were enough crackpots in the army to make me look normal. But I didn't give up, no way.

Faking madness was not a desire but a necessity. During my night duties, as a corporal in charge of the guards I had the keys to the company room and could sneak in to listen to the short-wave radio, to stations such as Radio Liberty from West Germany, Voice of America, and some Chinese stations. Communist China didn't tell me anything new, it had the same bashing propaganda as the Soviet Union which looked pink compared to the very red Maoists from Peking. But the Western journalists really stirred me up, sometimes I agreed with them, sometimes I didn't. One of their statements I remember by heart: "The Soviet soldier is an unsophisticated and relatively simple man. His conception of life is limited by his own experience, although he may be vaguely aware of life in other societies. Since he is unsophisticated and used to comparatively few comforts, he is an uncomplaining soldier, one accustomed to living a spartan life, a spartan existence - by Western standards. He makes a good line soldier, one who obeys without question and one who can live under relatively primitive conditions."

CHAPTER 7

There is nothing good in a man but his young feelings and his old thoughts.
Joubert

THERE WAS A GROWING CONFRONTATION BETWEEN ME AND the collective. Borzenko kept a close eye on my every move, making sure I would be the last one to go to bed at night and the first one to rise. Legally he was not allowed to give me overnight duties more than twice a month but adding little jobs here and there he secured my tiredness and longing for bed.

The only available fraction of free time was between lunch and homework, about 45 minutes, which I used to spend either snoozing in the Lenin Room or reading medical literature in the regiment library. It was a very good library. Many books and tall solid shelves hid me safely from the curiosity of the lady librarian - Galina Porfiryevna.

I didn't want to alarm her by my specific interest in everything relating to mental disorders - parapsychology, metaphysics, Eastern religions, classic and European philosophy. I would read one sort of book standing there near the stacks, but to check out I would grab different stuff - completely junky novels popular among privates. Luckily the library was far from crowded. Some of the young soldiers were attracted there simply to glance at Galina Porfiryevna who was a typical Russian beauty with a juicy voice and enormous breasts; her silhouette in her white woolen sweater resembled a world War II vintage bomber piercing a cloud.

CHAPTER 8

Go forth to meet the shadowy Future without fear.

Longfellow

THAT COMPULSIVE READING PROVIDED ME WITH SOMETHING I definitely lacked - the lexicon of a paranoiac, i.e. obscure words, and such extravagant ideas like the bending of time in the Theory of Relativity, Black Holes in Space, the mysteries of extinct dinosaurs, Egyptian pyramids, telepathy, etc.

Conspiratorialy bent over, going through tons of information literally within minutes, helped me to master a Diagonal method of speed reading - 5-6 seconds on any page however complicated the text is. You draw with your eyes a diagonal from the upper right corner of the page to the bottom left. Basically you gist instead of reading. You miss the literature's beauty but always get the main message.

One day I found Alyosha - the train boy - in the library. He wore the same sailor suit and was sitting in front of an open thick volume without in fact reading it. He just gazed melancholically above everything and didn't even notice me which I was pleased about; I didn't want to become the center of attention by saying hello to an unknown minor.

Gradually I reached that level of superficial knowledge when, like a Minister of Education in a third world country, I knew everything and nothing. I could support or initiate a conversation on any subject but wouldn't go deep and wouldn't last more than a couple of minutes. I learned through practice that the most striking nonsense came out of my mouth if I didn't know how to end a phrase and totally relied on inspiration, on the delicate guidance of the Spirit.

My poetic background came in handy. It made me think that such celebrities as biblical King David and the Roman Emperor Claudius scribbled love sonnets before they hid themselves from their deadly enemies in the jungles of false madness.

Sometimes right in the middle of a sentence I would get sweaty from fear that I had no idea how to continue it. But my slow speech and long pauses would give me just enough time to improvise the next delightful nonsense. I had no choice but to rely on a mysterious breeze from Heaven.

So here is the first warning.

PLEASE, if you are not a poet, stay away from this book, don't take any notice of my instructions. This Manual is a mountain road with collapsed bridges, you need wings and winds to survive on this road.

Of course, the most beneficial reading was from a bombastic Medical Encyclopedia (volume PSYC - SCHI), and a prerevolutionary edition of ' Guide for Countryside GPs'. I cleared my basic understanding of the widespread form of schizophrenia called PARANOIA: Paranoiacs often claim to have invented perpetuum-mobile, the eternal engine, or a chemical substance for turning cat's mess into shiny jewelry. They besiege academies and publishing houses with their essays, 'researches,' and amendments to the constitution. Resembling English snobs, paranoiacs try to trace their ancestors to modern or ancient kings, to abducted princes, to military geniuses such as Napoleon or Alexander the Great.

Paranoia can be aggressive or quiet, or both at the same time. I was happy with the parameters of this disease - you can accuse yourself for all the troubles in the world or on the contrary suspect everybody of persecution and attempts on your life. You can be melancholic, monosyllabic or a restless non-stop talker. You can harass people with boasting or gently hint with a triumphant smile that you are the hope and pride of mankind.

It seemed that as long as I came up with some ideas of grandeur, without repeating stereotypical examples from these books, and stuck to the mode of Vaska's behavior, I could feel safe, confident.

Also, in paranoia I decided to add to Vaska's awkwardness a touch of my own personality. He would talk about physical science even while hanging upside down in the gymnasium so, with God's help, my conversations would be as heavily loaded as logging trucks with long philosophical charades. For a poet it wouldn't be difficult since poetry and philosophy are as close as blood and sea water - they share the same taste, the salty taste of truth.

To my surprise I received another vital input from the dull newspaper 'Komsomolskaya Pravda'. There was an article about self-hypnosis and detailed instructions on how, by rhythmic repetition of certain words, to achieve substantial changes in your body. For instance, repeating 'my left arm is warm, the warmth is liquid pouring into my arm' a man can raise his body temperature by at least 1° C. There was also a list of expressions for relaxation, for reducing stress, for slowing down natural reflexes. That list provided me with a short cut to the control of my face and body muscles, to Vaska's zombiness and his agitated state.

I was excited. In a week I noticed progress. And more than that - I realized a new use for the self-hypnosis - to keep persuading yourself to believe in your crazy, made up ideas, to believe that the world is against you, to believe you are the only one who knows the truth.

It was an obviously dangerous walk along the very edge of the cliff of real madness. I was still not mad but was already not sane, that's why my acting had a touch of genuineness.

Let's be more technical.

HOW TO IMPROVISE PATHOLOGICAL BABBLING

1. Relax in your whole body. Breathe deeply and slowly. Relax in your mind. Soften your brain to the max - to the point of being a ripe Californian vegetable.

2. Right in the beginning of the conversation drop in a couple of obscure, pretentious words, preferably relating to the topic and build your talk ONLY on your associations with those words.

3. Stretch the zig-zag line of your associations as long as possible. The longer it is the further you go astray from the subject of discussion. Then you will stink of madness without going mad.

Of course, it sounds easier than it is.

The inertia of traditional, rational responses is strong and nagging, like a farmer's wife. It pulls you back to common sense, to predictable answers, to familiar logical patterns. Just say 'no' to it.

A good catalyst for my imagination was my sarcasm, my revengeful feelings towards the army and whole state.

For instance in talking to my superiors I would dig up forgotten terminology from military archives or from the slang of another branch. That's how I cooled off an angry lieutenant when he rebuked me for hesitation in rendering the salute.

"Are you blind, Papadin? Can't you see an officer?"

"I am sorry, Comrade Lieutenant... I am really sorry... I saw you coming... I started lifting up my hand.... but I guess the nerve responsible for the shoulder didn't send the right impulse.... It happens often with machines too... The wire in the ignition gets damaged, twisted, torn off... The statistics say it was the main reason the vehicle-mounted multibarrelled rocket launcher frequently didn't fire in Eastern Prussia... It takes time to establish the cause of a problem, doesn't it?"

"What are you talking about?"

"About saluting. We can salvo... we can dip the colors... we can fire broadsides... or can just lift up the right hand if the nerve works... if the nerve does not work then Eastern Prussia comes to my mind... and the installation for 132 mm rockets ...devilish fire...bloody Nazis deserved it... And your rank, Comrade Lieutenant, obliges you to believe so. It is your duty and not a choice to be a patriot."

"Cut it off! Get going! Who do you think you are?"

"Nobody, I accept it. It is the glory of some men to govern well and of others not to govern at all..Governing... Leading... Raising your voice... It's amazing that the Germans let that oneball monster rule over them...I mean Hitler. He had only one instead of two....He got wild with inferiority ...My God what a hurry he was in looking for an atomic bomb...He probably..Hah-Hah-Hah thought the atomic bomb would be a good replacement for his missing ball...Our rocket launcher arrived just in time ...nicknamed 'Katyusha'... and if not for the bad ignition and crafty allies...The Brits were lead by Churchill...Now he is in a wax museum... How many candles were melted to make his sculpture? They robbed the church, I guess.."

"They did not."

"What a Navy the Brits had, what a Navy!..Veer out the fore backstay, take the stern backstay! Back all astern! Weigh the anchor!"

"I said get moving! Show off! Back to your duties, you book worm! About FACE! March!"

CHAPTER 9

The strength of any plan depends on the timing.

Montaigne

BY THE END OF DECEMBER I HAD SUCCEEDED in irritating almost everybody in our platoon but none of them attributed the worsening of my personality to mental disease. Time came for more understanding, sophisticated company. I was ready to see the doctors. I felt confident enough to face them. I was ready to challenge those overeducated hypocrites.

On the 27th in my spare time I walked to the sick bay. Captain Kudashev, the doctor from the medical corps, had already gone home. The doctor on duty was his civilian assistant Olga Sergeevna. She was famous for her excessive make up. It was a mystery whether she was a pretty angel or an ugly witch. The sounds of her voice, wrapped in the purple grease of lipstick, flew towards me with coquettish vibration.

"What's your complaint, young man? You look a bit pale."

"I don't know."

"Why did you come then? Let me measure your temperature. Don't drop the thermometer, they're in short supply." My temperature was 37.5° C for many weeks due to the bronchitis and mild form of pneumonia I had caught in the train. But because of the shortage of beds in the sick bay (10 for 900 men) such temperature was considered to be normal.

"You are fine. Take this aspirin. Three times a day."

"Thank you."

"Did you want to say something?"

"No-no."

"You look like something is bothering you."

"Not really."

"Good-bye."

I nearly made a vague comment about the side effects of aspirin, suntan and life in a small town but chickened out at the last moment - as medical sergeant Orehov walked in with some question to Olga Sergeevna. A vulgar, terrible cynic - he would have interrupted me and made me look like a trickster not because of his suspicions but because he constantly slandered others and made provocative jokes. I didn't want it to happen. Even a hint of suspicion could kill my plan at this stage.

22

I knew I'd done the right thing by not trying to alarm the doctor with my mumbling but at the same time I got frustrated with the whole situation.

'How can I get a meeting with captain Kudashev? What excuse can I produce for my next visit to the sick bay? How many more days do I have to spend in active service?'

On my return to the barracks my anguish was doubled by the news about an accident involving Borka Koverda. Now for sure he was eligible for a discharge but not the way he had wanted... He had gotten into an argument with old soldiers from the Construction Battalion which was attached to the regiment for maintenance of the combat airfield. Those bandits used to rob us of our pocket money, wrist watches, breakfast sugar, Sunday cookies, newly issued winter gloves or parcels from home.

That day, after they learned about the arrival of a big shipment of New Year parcels to the 1st Company they invaded our barracks and went through the boxes choosing the most tasty things. None of the young soldiers, traditionally nicknamed 'meatscraps', dared to grumble. Neither did Borka ...until he noticed one of them holding a block of chocolate with an illiterate inscription from his grandma who brought him up instead of his parents (killed in an airplane crash).

So, without thinking, mesmerized by the familiar writing, he pulled the chocolate out of the hands of the old soldier and didn't even get a chance to explain himself - he was beaten and hit five times in the rear by the buckle of a swinging belt. Hitting in the rear with a buckle, spoon or empty bayonet holder is a non-official ritual called 'taking an oath'. That's how the old soldiers humiliate and punish rebellious 'meatscraps'.

But this time Borka was more than unlucky - the blows damaged rudimentary vertabrae at the end of his spine. He was immediately paralyzed from the waist down. He did not even feel the pain.

When they untied him he collapsed on the floor and all his attempts to get up turned into strange swimming movements - the movements of a tadpole before its legs grow. Borka was so frightened by his immobility that he refused to believe it and kept smiling up to the silent crowd.

"Hey, guys, can somebody give me a hand? What are you staring at, eh?"

CHAPTER 10

Life is a tragedy for those who feel, and a comedy for those who think.

La Bruyere

THAT DAY THE FACT THAT BORKA, LIKE ME, HATED the army; was, like me, a corporal; adored, like me, guitar music and fried potatoes, bent all my thoughts into one superstitious question - 'What if our similarities continue and bring me to the same tragic finale?

The more time I waste the more chances it might really happen. I should be more urgent about a discharge. But what should I do, what? How can I find out which day Captain Kudashev himself accepts appointments, talks to the sick and selects the patients? He is my only hope. I have to see him and cause alarm with my madness.'

"Please, Father, please" was my shortest, hottest night prayer. The huge dark ceiling of the dormitory was sliding from the sky like a negative of God's portrait... but his response was positive... He certainly heard my prayers but answered them in his usual ironic way - he pushed me to the limits of my physical and psychological capacity so making me more urgent about faking madness.

And this is how events developed.

The day after Borka Koverda was taken to the District Hospital, Sergeant Borzenko replaced him with a new leader for the Second team - Sheremetyev Shurka. Shurka was all right except for very inventive brown nosing. As I predicted, his promotion didn't decrease my duties and didn't shorten my nightshifts. The missing hours of sleep, like missing toes on both feet, made my walk unstable, wobbly. My night dreams, refusing to fade at the reveille horn, became more logical and real than reality.

The next time I was guarding the airfield at night I treated this life too carelessly, like a silly dream and ran into big trouble with military regulations: after marching sentries off to their posts, I thought, for no apparent reason, that I would take a little target practice. Why not? It was something I did routinely, with the safety on, so as not to disturb anybody. But in my befogged state of mind I forgot to disconnect the cartridge so instead of producing the harmless click I woke up the whole platoon with a long, loud salvo.

It was a ferociously frosty morning. But my platoon mates, thinking the Chinese had attacked us, rushed out of the guardhouse in their underwear, with bare feet, some without their automatic rifles. Borzenko, ready to lead the platoon in a counterattack, noticed my guilty face near the weaponry wall and canceled the alert. I knew I was dog meat; salted, canned, labeled.

As a punishment the major promised me three days in the district military prison which would not have been too bad. A short time later he decided to have mercy on me and changed his mind giving me 4(!!!!!!) 24 hour duties. I coped with the first one, then whispered to the mirror in the washroom 'BASTA!' That popular word of Italian origin had many nuances: 'I am out', 'I am done', 'get off my back', 'now or never.'

On the 6th of January, (Christmas Eve according to the calendar of the Russian Orthodox Church) while the platoon was marching to the mess hall, I threw myself right down on the snow and exhaled a long, long scream. My calculation was based on common sense: even in our army they couldn't ignore a soldier lying in pain.

The guys lifted me up and carried me to the sick bay, into the light, into the warmth, into the scary future. There, once again, was Olga Sergeevna. To see again her painted clownish face instead of Kudashev was too much for me. Sheer exhaustion and a fear of my own pushy impudence smashed the dashboard of my self-control. I burst into tears. Then realizing how beneficial my tears were to my psychotic reputation, how well they complemented my recent screaming, I started crying deeper, louder, but hiding my face in the towel as if I were embarrassed by my hysterics.

"What's wrong with you, Papadin? Did somebody die in your family? When was the last time you got a letter from your parents?"

I enjoyed not answering those silly perfumed questions. I enjoyed my privilege not to talk to anybody - the Royal privilege that accompanies the title of a madman.

More concerned than offended by my silence Olga Sergeevna arranged a bed for me in a small cozy ward. Nobody heard the whispered promise of Corporal Papadin. "I'll sleep till next Christmas. Only a fire or the Second Coming will drag me out of bed."

Naturally my sleep was shorter than that but still impressive - almost 60 hours - two nights, one day with small interruptions for the bathroom and Kudashev's questions 'What is the date today? What year? How many fingers on my hand?' I would give him a hazy glance before each answer. I didn't have any energy left for philosophical talks. The best I could do was an alien look and pathologically slow speech (my syllables crawled along my tongue in the miniature shells of newborn crabs).

I hardly ate anything. I was too sleepy and nervous to have an appetite. Too much was at stake. Some people can eat the day they bury their father. Their stomachs are not connected with their thoughts and feelings. Mine is.

CHAPTER 11

The last thing one knows...is what to put first.

Pascal

ON THE 8TH OF JANUARY KUDASHEV TOOK ME four hours by train from Spassk-Dalniy to the District Military Hospital in Ussuriisk, a middle-size city. He said he wanted to show me to another doctor, a specialist in cases similar to mine. The captain's clumsy secretiveness made it obvious to me that 'the specialist' was a psychiatrist. I quite liked the captain. He was soft-spoken and well-mannered - features hardly existing in my generation.

In Ussuriisk, near the railway station newspaper stand I met a familiar face - the non-talking boy Alyosha. This time he was dressed in warm, expensive clothes - sheep skin coat, matching hat, foreign winter boots. He was obviously from a wealthy family and lived in this city.

While Captain Kudashev got distracted by a money peddling group of gypsy women Alyoshka waved to me and smiled in such a way as if he knew what turbulences I had been going through for the last two months and why I was walking like a sleepy dummy.

This meeting cheered me up. Only I got a bit of an attitude to the unknown parents of Alyosha: with the money they had they could easily have taken better care of his forehead which was still bleeding.

The hospital consisted of many buildings, one for each department. The captain was leading me to the one behind a wooden fence.

Part II

ASYLUM IN A MADHOUSE

"The hospital consisted of many buildings, one for each department. The captain was leading me to the one behind a wooden fence."

CHAPTER 1

We learn to howl in the society of wolves.

Countess Du Barry

A FTER WE HAD GONE THROUGH THE MAIN ENTRANCE Kudashev left me in a small corridor, on a bench, in front of the office and went through the dark door lit up by glittering letters on a glass sign:

HEAD OF DEPARTMENT

MAJOR ZABUSOFF

'If that man's experience matches his high rank and expensive door sign, he will see through me immediately and arrest me even before the snow melts on my boots. But if he lets me talk, man, I won't hold back. I'll unload a truckload of nonsense into his brain and ears.'

Those few minutes were agonizing - as if I was sitting in a dentist's chair, being jacked up towards the shiny metal claws, bright neon lights, bright promise of pain.

"Come in, Papadin."

After letting me in, Captain Kudashev disappeared without saying good-bye, leaving me face to face with Destiny.

I made a shaky step inside the office in the careful manner of a blind man who has just dropped his walking cane. Also, to increase the effect of my pathological indifference to the world, I thoroughly defocussed my eyes as I used to do at home while watching purple sunsets above the roofs and remote mountains. As always, such defocussing led to two main illusions: some subjects, even immobile ones, started moving, and their sizes at least doubled. That's why I wasn't surprised to find myself under attack from a huge fast flying crow which suddenly put in reverse, hit the wall behind a wide oak desk and turned into the clean haircut of the chief psychiatrist whose shiny black hair resembled recently laid asphalt. His welcoming smile exposed a sign of a good steady income - at least two of his front teeth had gold crowns.

But the major was not alone. To the right side of the desk, in an antique armchair, there sat a lieutenant with brass medical snakes on his shoulder-loops, an assistant, without a doubt, who started and led our crucial conversation. To let the lieutenant be the leading interrogator was a very clever strategy of the psychiatrist. Not participating in the conversation,

"His welcoming smile exposed a sign of a good steady income - at least two of his front teeth had gold crowns."

Major Zabusoff was able to watch patients more attentively because one sees better when one doesn't talk. Also for any normal guy like me the presence of a silent foe would be very oppressive, provocative.

"Hello, Corporal. I am Lieutenant Bolotnikoff and you, I believe, are Papadin, Valentin. Military base # 62546. Correct?"

"Yes, sir."

"But now you are not in your regiment. You are here... Do you know where you are?"

"I am afraid I do."

"Where?"

"In hospital."

"Yes, in the psychiatric department... Tell me, please, what do you think brought you here?"

"Jealousy."

"I'm sorry?"

"Jealousy and conspiracy."

"Interesting."

"They envy me. They are choking with envy, that miserable bunch."

"Who's 'they?'"

"Everybody."

"Including your superiors?"

"Oh yes, they are the first ones to slander me. I've been the only target of their pathetic sense of humor. They kept me - ME!- in the kitchen. They sent me to guard an airfield with airplanes which never flew and never will. It's such a burden to be a genius, a pioneer in science and philosophy. Mediocrity cannot stand such people like me and Leonardo da Vinci."

"So you and Leonardo are buddies?"

"Please, Comrade Lieutenant, 'Leonardo' was a cat next door to my home. I am not an animal activist. Full names will do better - Leonardo da Vinci and Valentin Papadin."

"I see."

The lieutenant's irony made me very curious: what exactly did he look like? But it was not the right moment to scrutinize the faces of my foes. I still had a lot to say. I had to drive them nuts. They would never forget me. Both of them would put my color picture in their Ph.D. folders.

"Tell me, Valentin Papadin, when did you first notice everybody turning against you?"

"In boot camp, the day I discovered a Third Telepathic Eye in the back of my head."

"Third Eye?"

"Yes, sir."

"Third?"

"What's so surprising, Comrade Lieutenant? Every true genius carries visible physical marks of his superiority. Leonardo da Vinci was left handed, William Shakespeare was a woman, Lord Byron limped...you know. They all had beneficial abnormalities and I am like them."

After this last tirade I felt so much tension accumulated in my body and soul that I had to release it by crying or laughing. I chose crying as a more appropriate reaction in the situation.

"You know, Comrade Lieutenant, when I recollect the lives of these noble people and see how much I resemble them and share with them the bitter fate of being mocked and humiliated by ignorant compatriots, I can't help crying."

"That's all right, I understand."

There was a long pause while the lieutenant was scribbling notes in his note book. The chief psychiatrist, my main enemy, was quietly flicking a match-box along the edge of the desk. His intimidating silence crawled towards me on the slippery belly of a rattle snake. The yellow spark from his golden teeth could hit me at any moment. I had to be more aggressive. As our sergeant used to say 'The best defense is an attack.'

"Thank you, sir, thank you, Comrade Lieutenant. One day your sympathy will be rewarded."

"Valentin, you said the Third Eye is in the back of your head. Could you show it to us?"

"What's the point? You have to have your own Third Eye to see mine. Plus you don't even know it's main characteristic."

"What's that?"

"It's also a Time Machine. It enables my mind to travel in the Past and Future, just like that! One, two, three and I am right in the middle of a funeral procession of the Egyptian pharaoh Amenhotep # 53535628839."

Saying that, I was still not looking at the doctors. Instead my slow dreary distracted gaze, heavier than a bumble-bee, was knocking at the glass of the window, moving the curtains, scratching the ceiling but so far it hadn't landed where it was longing - on the forehead of Major Zabusoff.

Meanwhile I was dying to continue the chosen subject - Telepathy. I was well prepared for it. Not long ago I had read an article in a biology magazine about a mysterious hole in the foreheads of unearthed dinosaurs. The scientists speculated that the hole used to be a third, not properly developed eye which later refined itself as an organ of telepathy. But the most curious thing is that our human scalps also have a soft spot in the same place - between the eyes, on the eyebrow level. And there is also a strange knot of sensitive nerves in our brain right under the softness in the scalp. So we must also be telepathically active. In case the doctors too had read this article I 'moved' the telepathic center into the back of my head and added to it a ridiculous ability to function as a time machine. But the lieutenant suddenly switched to a trivial procedure - filling up forms.

"Valentin, there is a questionnaire, it helps us to figure out your needs."

"I need only paper to write down my latest theses. I have solved all of the most difficult problems which have bothered mankind since time immemorial. My sacred duty is to put everything down in writing."

This outward aggressiveness of mine was a consequence of an inner feeling of relief. I was pleased with the news about a questionnaire. The stupidity of Soviet bureaucracy, which compiled those questionnaires, would certainly provide me with plenty of time and space for self-control and imagination. Now I felt confident enough to look attentively at the doctors. Now it was time to add the arrogance of a glance to the arrogance of crazy babbling. I slowly moved my head in the direction of the oak desk. Major Zabusoff, flicking the match-box in the opposite direction, was exactly who he was supposed to be: a clean shaven, intelligent city doctor with the narrow black eyes of a money-making hypnotist. His obvious intelligence was an encouraging sign: such people suffer from boosted self-esteem and don't like to change their opinions. Once he decided I was a nut-case, he would stick to that decision and it would eventually become the basis for the official diagnosis.

The lieutenant represented another type of successful doctor: simple, relaxed, boyish. All 360 degrees of his round countryside face were full of frequent freckles and happy selfishness. He was definitely used by the major as an easy bait for tricksters like me. But my fear of the silent major was so strong that in my imagination his features were projected onto the lieutenant. So, in fact there were two majors confronting me in that office. Together these two were a strong team. Still, who could measure the power of my desperation?

"Comrade Lieutenant..."

"Excuse me, Valentin, we really have to get to these forms. Question #1: Do you ever wet the bed?"

"I can if I have to."

"Did you ever have homosexual affairs?"

"What is 'homosexual?'"

"Did you ever kiss boys, play with them, you know, in a funny way?"

"Do you mean forbidden games?"

"Exactly."

"Like cards, 'shells'?"

"Oh, forget it. Question #3: did you ever have seizures, concussions?"

"What?"

"Did you ever lose consciousness?"

"If I did how would I remember it?"

"How often do you play with your private parts?"

"I am not here..."

"What's your father's name?"

"Not here."

"Do you have nightmares? Black cats?"

"Sir, right now I am in the 16th century. Shall I describe to you the town square I am crossing now and the medieval fountain I'm throwing coins into?"

"That's enough for now, Michael Stepanich, thank you." The major finally walked into the conversation. "Glafira Hiccanorovna, could you please take the new patient to Ward #2?"

A broad shouldered woman (dressed in a lab coat and considered by my relaxed vision to be a white office refrigerator until she got up from the chair) led me to the shower room.

After the shower, with the shy smile of a chain smoker, orderly Glafira Hiccanorovna gave me some old but clean underwear, black faded slippers with soles made of car tires, and an old brown smelly dressing gown with the belt sewn into the waist at the back and with rusty crusts of dry blood in the wrinkles of the sleeves.

Then we went through two self-locking doors, reinforced along the edges with metal strips, into a dark green corridor full of noise, stink and mushroom-like pale faces.

"So, in fact there were two majors confronting me in that office."

CHAPTER 2

A man must swallow a toad every morning if he wishes to be sure of finding nothing still more disgusting before the day is over.

Chamfort

WATCH THE STEPS AND STICK TO ME FOR YOUR OWN GOOD or they will get you."

By 'they' Glafira Hiccanorovna was referring to the crowd of my new found peers wearing clumsy turbans made of undershirts. I didn't take her warning seriously until an amorphous hullabaloo gradually crystallized into a clear threat to my life.

"Fresh meat arrived! Newcomer! Hurry up, guys! Renew the menu! Let's all have a bite!"

It was the first time I had heard public acknowledgement that my body could appear appetizing. With whistling, barking, cockadoodledoing, sporadic breaking wind, the raving mad Zulus jerked me away from the orderly and started pinching my cheeks, biting my ears, pulling my hair, hitting my legs viciously with knotted towels...As frightened to death as I was, I still had not lost the ability to ask myself rhetorical questions.

'Why are they allowed to attack me? Why aren't these mental patients separated from each other? They will finish me off. Such monsters should be chained to a wall, kept in a cage, soaked in icy water. Is this the 20th century? Age of computers and soft toilet paper? Do these loose beasts have human names and will we sit in the same mess hall? How can I survive in this place a single hour

34

never mind a day or a week?'

Being pushed, hurt and scared I could easily have had a heart attack if my heart had been in its place, in the upper left corner of my chest. But it was not. That treacherous piece of flesh had moved out of my body somewhere far away, to a remote corner of the universe and had probably become another twinkling star, confusing local astrologists there.

"Papadin, where are you? Are you all right? Cut it out, boys, can't you see he is shaking?"

Glafira Hiccanorovna was slowly fighting her way back to me, cutting the crowd in two halves with the unstoppable power of an Arctic ice-breaker.

I suddenly fell in love with her macho voice. I enjoyed the sight of her protective corpulence. I found her emancipated crudeness erectionally sexy. I never knew that such women could turn me on but it was a day of many exceptions.

I followed Glafira Hiccanorovna lock step so closely that her lab coat was rubbing my nose and I was faithfully inhaling the exotic swampy smell of her sweating armpits.

"There is your bed, third on the left, with the bent headboard. Lie down and rest. My advice is not to wander around. These are not handkerchiefs but towels, one for face, one for feet. The towels are as short as this in our department because there are always fools who try to hang themselves. You are not allowed to have matches or razor blades. Do you hear me? Not allowed to lie in bed in a dressing gown - only under the blanket, in underwear. Not allowed to spend more then 10 minutes in another ward. Not allowed to smoke in the ward. Not allowed to enter the officers' ward under any circumstances. Not allowed to be late for meals. Next meal is at 7:30 P.M. Not allowed to bring food into the ward. Doctor's rounds are on Monday and Friday, at 10.00 A.M. Not allowed to be out of bed at that time. I'll bring your toothpaste, address-book and envelopes from the storage room tomorrow if the major permits. So long my little rabbit."

I didn't so much listen to Glafira Hiccanorovna as enjoy the minutes of ecstatic safety, provided by her closeness. I didn't want her to leave. But the white humungous iceberg (as big as the one fatal for the 'Titanic') inevitably moved away down the corridor following the undercurrent of its duties.

I lay in bed under the dusty woolen blanket, on my back, for better observation, hating the very thought that I didn't have archangel's wings or anti-infantry grenades or at least a humble hat of invisibility.

There were a dozen beds in the ward, six on each side. Most of them were undone and empty - a disturbing indication that the absent folks belonged to the Welcoming Committee and would be back all at once any minute.

Several inmates, woken up from their afternoon nap by the orderly's preaching, looked at me with brief curiosity, then again smashed their faces against their pillows with a bitter expression of deadly boredom that made any Russian idiot look like Solomon or Buddha or Confucius.

A cold draft from the corridor was making a smooth U-turn near my cheek. The interior of the ward presented a good example of the socialist style of furnishing - there was no furniture at all except for brown plywood bed cabinets, one for two inmates. There was no door at the ward's entrance either. I looked into the rectangular darkness of the entrance and wished I was blind and couldn't see the approaching mugs.

CHAPTER 3

*Passion often turns the cleverest man into an idiot and the greatest
blockhead into someone clever.*

Francois, Duke de La Rochefoucauld

THE WELCOMING GROUP STOPPED IN THE AISLE NEAR my bed. Three of
them moved closer. The most pale blockhead - with spasmodic body
movements and a languid look of an occasional child molester - sat
partly on me, partly on my bed, trapping my hand under the blanket.

"What's your name? Why are you here, in Ward #2? Did you kill
somebody?"

The questions Blockhead asked didn't help me to feel at ease. It
seemed I was in a bad neighborhood.

"What's your name? Talk, don't make me mad."

"Valentin."

"Good, very good. Tell us, Valentin, how it happened that you got
in such a mess."

"What mess?"

"Bedlam. To be honest, it's the slummiest place on earth. But we
are all special here. I stoned an officer. Gosha stole and sold tons of
explosives to some Korean fishermen who, in fact, were reconnaissance
men from a Chinese tank battalion. He might be shot for high treason.
Misha raped an officer's wife and their pet goat. Slava tried to burn the
headquarters of the Division newspaper: the bastards refused to publish his
poems - impressive stuff, you can appreciate yourself... Come on, Slava,
make me sad, read us your latest."

I didn't expect to find a poetic rival here. On the other hand, a mad
house is the most likely place to accommodate poets. A short blue-eyed
Slava was visibly moved by the attention. His nervousness, like summer
nettles, left fresh red scars across his face.

> "The army asylum in Ussuriisk
> laugh, but you'll be risking death,
> today it's Gomorrah and it's Sodom tomorrow
> and always it's sodding Gomorragh..."

"Is that it?"

"I have not finished it yet. I've had a bad cough."

"Get out of my sight, you sponge. Work harder and rhyme all verses, no cheating. Now you, Valentin, tell us loudly, what you have done."

"Nothing. I am a philosopher."

"Philosopher? Oh no, not another nut-case. Listen, Philosopher, can you box?"

"No, I can't."

I gave a false confession to Blockhead. I had been through boxing-training for a year before being enlisted. I didn't tell the truth because I was afraid they would start testing me. But it was a wrong move. The restless inmates did not bother good fighters as much as mummy's boys. If I had told them about my strong uppercut, straight left and swing I could have avoided many painful hours.

"It's nice of you not to be a boxer. I am simply tired of hooligans", complained Blockhead in mock mourning.

He made himself more comfortable on my tummy and began to pat me softly on both cheeks like a fond father playing with his little son. His eyes were festering badly, making him squint and me choke with disgust. I moved my head away from his repulsive fingers and tried to free my left hand for better self-defense.

I was trapped and helpless, like my left hand under the blanket. At some point I thought that maybe I had died that day, that morning, on the train to Ussuriisk but had failed, as happens with many corpses, to close my eyes at the moment of death, and now, with a dead body but still living vision, I was watching a life unfold in which I had no interest anymore.

My passive resistance to Blockhead made him more happy than angry. He shouted over his shoulder.

"Attention, crew, Philosopher tried to kill me. He must be punished. Who saw how he tried to kill me?"

"We all did. He's so wild."

"He also called me dirty names."

"Oh yes, he did. We are witnesses."

"What punishment does Philosopher deserve?"

"Two pints of blood. From each heel."

"When do we suck the blood?"

"At midnight, as always."

"All right, Philosopher, we'll be back later."

The picture of somebody drinking my blood in 1969, in the country of superior culture and the highest living standards in the world, seemed too grotesque to believe. The guys couldn't be serious.

They were certainly overplaying their cannibalism, I was sure. On the other hand with their teeth and enthusiasm any bite would be painful, even as a joke. That's why that night I made sure I was the last one in the ward to fall asleep - an easy thing to do for many reasons.

Eerie blue light bulb above the entrance... stamping steps and constant smoking of the male orderlies...acid smell of chlorine and water disinfecting the cement floor... snoring of my neighbor on the right... the eyes of Blockhead half open, like moldy mussels, ...my own thoughts, chaotic, fearful, leaning in all directions like gravestones in a village cemetery.

CHAPTER 4

It's good manners to join in what everybody is doing.

Stendhal

T HE VERY FIRST DAY IN THE PSYCHIATRIC DEPARTMENT provided me
with unforgettable impressions for the rest of this life and the next one
to come. It didn't take me long to figure out exactly where I was.

I was in big trouble. About half the inmates definitely fitted the
definition of raving mad. The other half, more dangerous for me, could be
called sane and violent, if sanity and violence don't exclude each other.
They were the soldiers who had committed various crimes of an awkward
nature and were sent here by court martial for observation, to verify their
sanity before final judgment. A period of observation, approximately two
weeks, were their last days of modest comfort, and relative freedom. They
knew they couldn't avoid the Military Tribunal, located in the city of
Habarovsk, on the Amur river. Harsh military prison was an approaching
reality. They ate and slept with a tummy ache of fear and, in turn, tried to
make our lives as sour as possible.

The specter of a long prison term wriggled around their heads like
a paper dragon in a Chinese carnival. Such guys, in hysterical inspiration,
hurried to have as much fun as possible. They turned that Bedlam into an
amusement park where lunatics paid for everything. To be in here meant to
be terrorized and humiliated all day long.

The ringleaders among the fun-and-games boys were hardened
criminals, ex-cons or drug addicts, whose thirst for unavailable drugs, on the
one hand, deepened their depression, and on the other hand, boosted their
wicked energy.

During Stalin's rule men with criminal records were not allowed to
enlist but the regulation changed after Nikita Krushchev's last trip to Europe
and his brief shoe campaign in the conference hall of the United Nations.
Krushchev, the famous Russian redneck, was alarmed by the wealth and
good manners of Westerners. He considered their hospitality to be proof of
their conspiracy and decided to toughen up the Soviet Army by recruiting
hooligans, thieves, murderers and other kinds of idealists. Whether he
achieved his goal or not I don't know, but his policies for sure had a direct
impact on a variety of inmates and on the cultural routine in our remote,
Far-Eastern, God-forsaken army asylum...

By law Major Zabusoff was given 15 days to assess the mental state of each soldier. A third week of hospital confinement automatically suggested that you were mentally sick and your discharge papers were being processed. It was extremely useful to know.

It meant I had to do my best only for two weeks and then to take it easy.

'But can I survive to the end of my observation? Can I - without turning, from beating, into an idiot or an invalid? Without a nervous breakdown? Without running to the major with a suicidal confession? Can I?'

The problem was - the crazier my speech the harsher the treatment I'd get from Blockhead's gang. 'But do I have a choice? No, I don't. I have to act as a paranoiac to the best of my ability in front of every single mug because in this jolly country informers are everywhere, even in a mortuary freezer.'

I had to watch myself constantly because the nurses kept a track of all our fights, incidents, comments and attitudes, in a thick, greasy 'Observation Note-book'. The echoing draft in the corridor brought the nurses all news about our private lives.

CHAPTER 5

Society is composed of two large classes; those who have more dinners than appetite, and those who have more appetite than dinners.

Chamfort

THE NURSES' USUAL OBSERVATION POST WAS A CHUNKY bench at the entrance to the officers' ward. That ward was roomy and had only seven beds and five officers. Two officers were clearly cuckoo. Three others were chronic alcoholics, tormented either by hallucinations or by letters from angry wives and creditors.

The officers had little luxuries we were not entitled to: a small radio on the wall and painted bars on the window. Their smart hospital uniforms also indicated the social structure within our army: warm flannel jackets, custom sized trousers, home slippers, handkerchiefs.

The only fridge in the mess hall belonged, of course, to the same elite. Warmhearted officers' wives supplied their husbands with tasty goodies we ordinary soldiers had forgotten or had never known: Estonian cheese, smoked sausage, tinned apricots, chocolate, cookies with raisins etc.

What could my three rubles a month do against the 250-270 rubles of an officer's salary? Never mind the money, we didn't even have buttons on our underwear flies. That's why if we, for instance, were all beheaded by Chinese reconnaissance men, the orderlies and nurses would still recognize us - by the color of our pubic hairs, to say the least.

Still, the upsetting issue wasn't so much the contents of the refrigerator as the way the officers, sitting in the same mess hall, shoveled up or savored those delicacies right under our noses. It was one of many reasons why dirty dressing gowns hated flannel jackets. That's how bloody revolutions start - with the smell of someone's food stretching in the air above your empty plate.

The cleanest, sunniest and sanest ward was #1. In that ward I wouldn't have had so many environmental problems. The crazy lot here were touched by schizophrenia in a quite acceptable, tolerable way and a couple of sane guys were there just waiting for the end of their observation period. One guy, from Moscow, could never stop smiling, and for his unwashable expression of happiness was nicknamed 'Yanky'.

An old soldier with a fluffy hairy chest, neck and ears had an unbelievably high temperature (+40° C) without any trace of physical or mental disorder and without feeling bad or hot.

Also a curious case was an infantry man who didn't feel any pain. Even a cigarette burning his palm he referred to as 'tickling'.

Ward #3 gave me a really gruesome impression. That ward was a home of madness, a castle of despair, dark, stuffy, filthy, stinky.

One guy, Vova, avoiding numerous assassins and creatures from another dimension, ate and slept right on the floor under his bed, and climbed out only to get a drink or to have more room for masturbation.

Ilyushka Steam-Engine was a tireless jogger in the department corridor. He was chased by herds of angry voices. The only thing which could slow him down was a gift of a cigarette - a great treat for a penniless smoker, a treat crossing the border of his insanity.

Small and fragile Little Tartar entertained us by tearfully begging: 'Shoot me, I am a traitor, I don't want to be a soldier, shoot me by firing squad!' It was uncomfortable for me to see the parallels between someone's madness and my secret thoughts and feelings. For instance, the pleas of Little Tartar eerily expressed the exact timbre of my occasional subconscious guilt towards my country and platoon mates whom I had deserted and left for dead if a war between Russia and China started...

Andrey Arbusov acted as a self-proclaimed witch-doctor. He would start the day by cursing inmates one by one, in order of beds, and then, to save them from those evil spells, he would sprinkle with his urine all blankets in the ward - all except his own.

Round faced, with scars and muscles of a Roman gladiator, maniac Matvey was tied to the bed frame with twisted sheets because of his attempt, almost successful, to strangle his neighbor, psycho hypochondriac Vadim. To be fair to Matvey I have to admit that he tried to do to Vadim what the majority of inmates felt like doing.

Vadim spent all his spare time (14-15 hours a day) following us around with the merciless determination of Jehovah's Witnesses and declaring the same nagging revelation 'We are dead, dead, dead.' Perhaps, before losing all screws from his brain's bracket Vadim had been obsessed with men's illusory mortality, so later Satan used that obsession as a fertilizer for full blown madness.

Death was certainly not a favorite subject to be mentioned in our catacombs - it was on our minds anyway.

In the daylight we had a bunch of restless con-men with knives made of sharpened spoon handles. And at night, when the nurse started dropping her head in a snooze, we were vulnerable to each other's dreams and madness. For instance, on my second night my neighbor on the left, an artillery sergeant with epilepsy, nicknamed Belly-Robber, woke me up not saying a single word - he just stood near my bed and stared at me with his big watery eyes and the indecisive expression of an entomologist who doesn't know whether to pin a butterfly to the cardboard or to dip it in boiling plastic preservative.

And when I closed my eyes pretending I was not scared and ready to continue sleeping he shook my shoulder again. Although he left me alone after that, my beating heart kept me awake for quite a while.

CHAPTER 6

Men often choose to love those they fear, in order to be protected by them.

Joubert

MY THIRD DAY WAS SPENT IN A USELESS search for a safe spot. Even sitting on a bench in the corridor, two yards from the nurse didn't prevent me from being hit in the jaw. I was hit by a petty criminal from Barnaul - for no reason at all. He just approached, bent down and hit me. The stone wall behind me doubled the impact.

When I regained consciousness he was already gone. (Was it an incident or a short dream about long pain?)

Hitting somebody, preferably 'an idiot', for no reason, was a common practice. It had a spicy touch of absurdity. For both sides it was a brand new experience. Demons of boredom ruled the normal guys and competed in nastiness with the demons of the raving mad.

There was neither chess nor checkers in the wards. It was too expensive to keep replacing them. The only set of dominoes had been swallowed, piece by piece, by a heroin addict who, playing for time and postponing a trip to the Habarovsk Tribunal, thus provided himself with a transfer to the surgery department.

Among made up games the most popular was 'CUTTING OFF THE OXYGEN'. Three or four of the sane ones would sneak up behind some unsuspecting victim, and two of them would hold his arms while a third suffocated him with a wet towel bound over his nose and mouth. The wetness prevented air from getting through; it could also be used to deliver heavier blows to the victim's neck after the main entertainment was finished.

The victim would try to get free, but the fun-and-games boys would just look him in the face and continue stifling him until he fell limp and his eyes grew bloodshot. I dreaded this trick. I was never comfortable if there were more than two people standing behind me. But many had to go through it, and I, too, had my oxygen turned off at the end of my third day.

They caught me in the ward while I was standing in sweet philosophical melancholy in front of the window, and wrapped the towel around my nose and mouth in spite of my struggles. It hit me really badly. While wrestling wildly in an attempt to break free I became soaked in sweat but couldn't escape.

Before I blacked out I spotted my reflection in the double glazed window - my bulging face was pulsing with purple and blue like a finger nail slammed in a door.

When I came around they were holding my arms and laughing at me because the fear and tension had made me wet myself .

"Among made up games the most popular was 'CUTTING OFF THE OXYGEN'."

CHAPTER 7

Fools are more dangerous than foes.

Russian Proverb

O N THE FOURTH DAY, IN THE MESS-HALL, Belly-Robber had a chance to justify his nickname......For breakfast there was omelet, his favorite dish. So he took my plate, spat in the middle of my omelet, then gave it back to me.

"Eat it, pal, and in case you don't I sure can."

Of course, I didn't. My appetite was killed at close range. But not Belly-Robber's. He shoveled up my omelet, that golden shaky dream, with disgusting speed.

Ooh, I hated him. I hated him more for waking me up three nights in a row. I hated him for picking on me as if he belonged to the superior club, the Blockhead gang, though he didn't. He was one of us, 'the idiots'. He had epilepsy in such a heavy form that it penetrated even his voice-box - he stuttered, especially before or after seizures.

I also hated that punk from Barnaul for that treacherous blow. I hated those two delinquents for nearly choking me to death in a 'turn off the oxygen' game.

Surprisingly, I didn't hate Blockhead himself and a couple of other ex-cons because, in my opinion, they had already moved out of the area of human reasoning or feeling, into the category of those simple glowing water organisms with which life started on earth. I was afraid of them, and nothing else.

But my relationship to the guys possessing at least a fraction of humanity could be classified only as hatred. I also hated the major and his assistants for their indifference to our rotten routine, to the dangers we were exposed to.

CHAPTER 8

It is the glory of some men to write well and of others not to write at all.
La Bruyere

S O FAR I HAD SEEN THE DOCTORS PRECISELY TWICE after the first interview, on Monday and Friday mornings, when they were making ward rounds. They moved fast, accompanied by the senior nurse and a male orderly, spending 7 seconds near each bed. I hardly managed to remind them about a note-pad for my theses.

They promised it and I was happy, I felt like a million rubles. A note-pad would be the perfect place to keep my sick philosophy. There I could be as mad as I had to without winding up Blockhead and the same time provide Major Zabusoff with solid grounds for my discharge. But when, on Friday, a pretty nurse called Natasha brought me a small note-book and pencil, I didn't know what to write.

My crazy spontaneous babbling was never a product of wit, it was a shaking, timid child of my fear, it was inspired by the real faces of my numerous enemies. But here, on paper, I got stuck with sterilized silence and unlimited, uncomfortable freedom.

As a professional poet and amateur nutcase I was totally lost in the vast spaces of prose. Plus I never remembered Vaska Ryabuhin putting anything in writing. His madness was strictly spoken. So I didn't have a pattern to follow. What a fool I was! Asking for paper I asked for troubles and got them!

I spent in vain a good portion of Friday in bed, chewing the bitter, dead wood of the pencil and x-raying the walls and inmates with my empty, unfocussed glance.

Finally my creative silence got on Blockhead's nerves. He ducked under his bed, grabbed a slipper and threw it in my direction. The slipper missed me but the question didn't.

"Hey, there, why are you staring at me?"

"I am not."

"Are you trying to say I am not worth looking at?"

"I didn't say that."

"Watch yourself."

"I do."

"No you don't. You look at me as if you know everything."

"I sure do."

"Nonsense."

"I know everything even when I don't."

"What's that supposed to mean?"

"I can find an answer to any question. But not on an empty stomach. Belly-Robber steals my food."

"You yourself give it to him."

"Well, after he spices it..."

"Tell me, if you know everything, what is 'sake'?"

"Japanese rice vodka."

"Right... Still, you can't know everything...Listen, Philosopher, who in your opinion is more clever - you or me?"

"Mmmm."

"Who?"

"Mmmm.."

"Come on, be honest."

"Me."

Naturally, it wasn't an easy answer. I had openly challenged the ringleader. If I didn't have to act as a paranoiac I would have praised Blockhead, that stupid cruel imbecile, for his brilliant mind, good manners and meekness, but I had to stick to my role, and, since paranoiacs never compromise, never give up monopoly on superiority, I also had to put myself above absolutely everybody.

I reasoned wisely: two or three blows from him would not hurt me as much as the reputation of a compromiser in my self-evaluation... Everything adds to my public image, everything goes into my file on the psychiatrist's desk.

The blows arrived, more than three, and much later, at night, when I was fast asleep. That night's beating was one of the worst experiences in my life.

When I was hit the first time I didn't know what it was, I didn't know who I was, I didn't know that me (who was me?) was really me. When I was hit again and again I started realizing that that strange rising heat in my body was called Pain. But that understanding of pain was not clear at all because I still had not been woken up. Those hard fists threw me from my sleep straight into pain, not giving me a chance to wake up, to realize what was going on, not giving me time to remember that I had a voice and could call the orderlies for help.

My squirming, wriggling mind, like an unwanted human fetus during an abortion, had been dragged by blows from warm cozy darkness into painful darkness with an aftertaste of sterilized metal.. and the promise of the light which I saw ahead of me crumpled into nameless shadows of men who were as big as mountains and were very busy doing something terrible to me, something which separated me from myself and from the blurry treacherous light until the Judgment day, until the day of real light, when suddenly matured fetuses, dressed in long black robes, with silver powdered wigs, will turn all existing tables on the planet into drums with their angry wooden hammers.

After my night visitors had returned to their beds, finished talking and fallen asleep, I got up from bed. On the way to the toilet to rinse blood from my face and ears I made a kind of ski mask from a towel, so that the nurse on duty wouldn't notice any trace of beating. If she did learn about the incident and guessed about the involvement of Blockhead and Co., then, because of night time and the absence of witnesses, I wouldn't have been able to prove to him that I didn't rat, so my days of sound physical health would have been literally numbered.

I decided to reschedule my business hours, to move them to the evening and early night, when the inmates were mellowed by digestion of supper, by dusty blue dusk, when it was difficult to spot the direction of my glance.

During Saturday and Sunday nights I filled four pages with a wild mixture of scientific formulas and paraphrased, unrecognized proverbs and aphorisms of famous people. I didn't like the result very much. As I suspected my writing didn't have that head spinning charm of spontaneous madness, it was too heavy, sometimes too clever, sometimes too absurd. It looked fake. So it was. Instead of being a test-tube of my insanity that note-book could easily become my own epitaph.

I had to get rid of it and I did - shredded the pages into small pieces like tram tickets, and flushed them down the toilet.

I knew, watching the other psychos, that the destruction of certain papers or items can be evidence of psychosis: an uncontrollable need for secrecy. So my act was justified by the rules of my game. I could calmly confront the psychiatrist with empty hands and a significant smile.

On Monday, from the 'Observation Note-book', Major Zabusoff understood that my intensive writing was interfering with my sleep. That day I was put on a medication usual for this block - aminazine, two green pills, a very strong tranquilizer so acid that to rinse it down and also to prevent heartburn each patient was given a small glass of boiled milk. I didn't like the idea of getting medication but swallowed the aminazine out of curiosity. It knocked me out almost immediately, it stole my mind from me the way the devil steals our souls - without any hope of their return. I can't remember what woke me first - a blasting headache or friendly hands dragging me to the mess hall for breakfast.

I got worried: aminazine, because it made me sleep so deeply, left me absolutely unprotected after lights out. How could I know where the inmates would be led by their nocturnal sense of humor? So in the evening I tried to skip medication, to trick Natasha by hiding pills under my tongue, but, as a newcomer, my mouth was double checked, and I was given a second cup of milk - this time to rinse down not little lies but little bitter pills.

My attempt to avoid taking medication was the main subject of a report to the head of the department who reacted traditionally - from Wednesday I started receiving injections of aminazine, once a day, 2 cubic centimeters of thick transparent liquid.

After the first injection, when my body had not adjusted yet to the sophisticated poison, I couldn't make it from the nurse's room to the ward - I collapsed in the corridor, my nose broke against someone's knee. I desperately tried to keep my eyes open, my heart was beating violently and I was conscious of an acute, vomit-inducing fear for my life.

I am still puzzled what kind of a drug aminazine is, what it consists of if it knocked me down within 2-3 seconds and was so slow to dissolve in spite of my daily rides on a hot water bottle. Evenly distributed between two buttocks, six lumps of undissolved aminazine, each the size of a pea hen egg, represented six days of a very painful week. My backside was so numb I had to sleep on my stomach.

Plus it was a masochistic act to go to the toilet because sitting upright was the most painful position.

The effect of the drug lasted for many hours, from the early evening, when they stuck me in the rear, almost to lunch time the next day. Then somehow I would come to my senses but basic, animalistic ones. Long sentences, clever speech, a quick reaction to someone's joke was a difficult task, almost impossible. I would spend the rest of the day until the next injection in bed, hugging the mattress and dreaming about the time when I would be able to lie on my back for as long as I wanted, forever, to be precise.

Aminazine added to my life plenty, but didn't take away much. It still left me with the thundering, desperate question 'Do the doctors believe my madness or not?' The fact that I was put on medication didn't mean a thing.

'Of course, there is a good possibility that my act is convincing and I am considered to be a patient in need of medical treatment. On the other hand these injections could be just a type of punishment - either for my discovered but not announced trickery or for something else I am not aware of.'

Massive doses of psychotropic drugs, like, for instance, 'sulfadiazine,' were used in our department as a punishment for both lunatics and sane but more often for the sane since they were the ones who usually started a brawl.

CHAPTER 9

It is difficult to free fools from the chains they revere.

THAT SUNDAY, LUCKILY FOR ME, DEFENSELESS ZOMBIE, THREE active guys, including Blockhead, received shots of sulfadiazine. They were stripped naked, tied to the bed's iron base with twisted sheets and injected with several 'cubics'. Several hours later they were untied because by that time they were totally harmless - they trembled in high fever, moaned with muscular pain and could not even pick up a blanket if it fell on the floor.

The next day food was brought to them in bed but they didn't touch it. They drank a lot - tap water and apple juice. They lost a lot of weight. They needed help to walk to the toilet. Their eyes were as hollow as Rasputin's.

It took them a week for full recovery. The funny thing was that for once they were not responsible for that particular brawl. I knew who the instigator was - a nut from Ward #3, an anonymous newcomer who visited our ward and offered to demonstrate his ability to move things by concentration of his will. He climbed onto a bedside cabinet, frowning and puffing his cheeks in a slobbering growl until the audience got fed up and started throwing pillows, slippers and pieces of soap at him.

The performer vanished but the mayhem escalated, growing with every passing minute, until all hell broke loose - the sane inmates and the lunatics who were not totally divorced from the world were overwhelmed by mass hysteria. I stayed in bed but gladly joined the choir, yelling as loud as possible, exercising my idle throat, getting rid of the unhealthy quietness which had accumulated in my lungs after weeks of passive drug-dimmed breathing and half-whispering.

I could do anything I wanted to. Nobody cared. Nobody watched me. Everybody was fully engaged in redecorating the asylum. The windows were smashed, beds piled up in the doorway, guys were pushing, hitting and chasing weaker fellows - using this short period of anarchy for their personal vendettas as always in Russia because the dream of a slave is never happiness and freedom but an opportunity to enslave and spit on others.

Nervous orderlies and warders fled from the mayhem to get reinforcements - military patrol and medical assistants from other parts of the hospital. They also called the doctors at home but only got hold of a lieutenant who arrived ten minutes later, furious and a bit drunk.

With a long shiny syringe, filled with yellow sulfadiazine, the cursing lieutenant looked like a space warrior after a rough landing on a hostile planet.

CHAPTER 10

The first days of a tyrant's death are the happiest days for the nation.
Roman Historian

THOSE DEVASTATING INJECTIONS TO BLOCKHEAD AND HIS bodyguards provided our ward with a relatively peaceful week which I couldn't enjoy much because of the increasing lumps in my buttocks. I dreaded going to the toilet. Finally the rear pain and tension caused severe constipation. I limped in clumsy panic to the senior nurse, explained to her the delicate position I was in, and through her compassionate interference, during the next round, the major spent about five minutes talking to me, canceled my injections but took from me a promise to behave, not to avoid oral medication.

"By the way Papadin, I bet you are running out of paper. Let me see what you've written so far."

"I destroyed the diary."

"Come on."

"It's true."

"You are kidding, aren't you?"

The major's disappointed face gave me a fright. Maybe I should have left him a couple of pages for Saturday evening instead of the crossword?

"C-c-comrade Major, you sh-sh-sh-ould check his mattress, mad people often use mattresses for storage..."

The unusually sweet stuttering of my neighbor Belly-Robber would have attracted millions of garbage flies if it were a summer season. The major asked me to get up and together with the lieutenant, flipped the mattress over and of course found nothing.

"Where did you hide your note-book?"

"I destroyed it. If my telepathic formulas fall into the wrong hands the consequences would be disastrous for the entire world. But, please, don't give up on me, I am planning to send a coded synopsis of the diary to Kiev university. You will hear about me! Sooner than you think."

"My aunt lives in Kiev...Why did you choose that city? Moscow university has many more facilities."

"Agreed. But there is a theological college only in Kiev. My philosophy is a cross between science and religion...Comrade Major, to send a synopsis by registered mail I need 10 roubles, could you, please, lend me that amount ?"

"We'll talk about it next time."

"You can give me two fives or three threes and a rouble..."

"Next time, I said."

It seemed to me our conversation went smoothly, but four days later, around 10 A.M., when I was standing at my philosophical post near the window, the nurse on duty tapped my shoulder.

"The boss wants you. In the office. Let's go."

"Who wants me?"

"Major Zabusoff, head of the department, in case you forgot."

The corridor draft, which had been entwining my feet, suddenly made a freezing circle around my jumping heart. (When news is scary I always hear it first with my body and only then with my head).

I followed the nurse, muttering a mixture of autogenic commands and pathetic self-pity, 'Be calm, calm, calm like a cup of camomile tea..No reason to worry...not yet...It can't be an arrest, no military patrol at the main door... And the nurse doesn't look like she's hiding any nasty surprises... Oh my God, I am really getting tired of this life...When did all this mess start? With the draft notification? No, much earlier, when my parents arranged for a female egg to be burglarized at night by a prowling male spermatozoon and gave my name to that intimate crime...Calm down, Valentin, calm down, drown yourself in nirvana of indifference...'

CHAPTER 11

Women can only be made to laugh by making them think as little as possible.

Stendhal

THE OFFICE WAS AS NOISY AS AN ENGINE ROOM ON A SHIP, smelled like a haidresser's salon and was crowded with guests, but not from the military tribunal. A smiling Major Zabusoff sitting at the desk, was flanked by more than a dozen good-looking, young, cheerful girls, dressed in white cotton jackets over their colorful sweaters - obviously students from a local medical college come here for an excursion as a part of training.

When all of them noticed my presence, a soft respectful silence unrolled between us like a Persian carpet with fluffy tassels.

"Good morning, Valentin, how are you doing to-day? "

"Better than ever, Comrade Major. Thank you for asking."

Instead of looking at the major's face, I stared at a framed photo of the Minister of Defense, Grechko, hanging on the wall. This helped make my glance more in character, indifferent, cool, dazed. I tried not to blink for as long as I could, as if my eyelids were paralyzed by deep thinking.

"I hope you don't mind us having a chat as old friends. Aren't we friends, Valentin?"

"If you say so."

"Honored, most honored ... I hope you still remember when and where you were born"

"June 15, 1951, Magnitogorsk, Urals mountains, the frozen side of the planet. I was born and I deeply regret it, my life became a misery after that reactionary mediocrity, calling themselves university professors, opposed everything I said or wrote. Finally they put me here, with lunatics, who don't know their ABC's and never brush their teeth."

"I see. Did you have good grades at school?"

"Never cared about it. Superficially speaking I was an ordinary boy, like many others until my time came."

"Until now ?"

"You said it, not me."

"Do you have repetitive nightmares - black cats, for example, or somebody is chasing you or strangling you?"

"Are you serious, Comrade Major? My dreams are sweet. I have nightmares when I wake up and look around."

"What don't you like in our department? Warm blanket, bed, three meals a day, completely free medical service. In capitalist countries you would file bankruptcy after the twenty days you spent here."

"I don't want to be here."

"You think your hospitalization is a mistake, don't you?"

"Yes, in regards to justice it is a mistake, but on behalf of those envious bookworms, who cannot stand me, it was a well calculated trap. In their shoes I would have done the same. The best way to silence opposition is to announce its insanity."

"You think you are a victim ..."

"...A victim of an international conspiracy. Precisely that."

"And we should let you out ?"

"Sir, how can I put it, without hurting your self-respect and rules of subordination? You can keep me in these grotty catacombs for a month, for a year, for ten years...That's all right, I'll accept it. I am patient with ignorant people."

After my last comment the room was filled with a high frequency noise like a rubber sponge being squeezed, though nobody was washing the office window - it was the suppressed giggling of the medical students who politely covered their lips with their unbelievably clean, fragile fingers.

"You are too sarcastic to-day, Valentin."

"No, sir, it's the other way round."

"Is it really?"

"You think I am a madman. Well, well, let's check History. All pioneers of science and philosophy were considered to be mad at first."

My non-stop impudence sparked off a new spree of giggling. The girls were too young and unprepared to keep in line with professional seriousness. I was still looking at the glossy nose of the Minister of Defense when I noticed out of the corner of my eye that the shrink was frowning disapprovingly at the students and wagging his index finger as if to say, 'You mustn't mock the afflicted.'

His secret admonishing meant only one thing - Major Zabusoff took me for real!

Hurray!!! He!!! Took!!! Me!!! For Real!! Completely poker-faced, I nearly yelled from happiness inside. I felt I was home and dry. I was dying to join the girls' giggling as a star of the show, as a dirty, unshaved cheerleader.

I was vibrating inside from joy. I was ready to burst with loud wild laughing. I had to stop breathing in order prevent it. I tensed my stomach muscles to stop the vibration of approaching happy hysterics. My throbbing heart had been tickled from inside with many flying feathers as if it were a boy's bedroom after a pillow fight.

I hadn't laughed properly for months. I needed it. My soul needed a laugh. My body needed a laugh. My tired brain cells needed a laugh.

I could not imagine a more funny thing than this pretentious stupid office where all of us were gathered for one purpose - to hide from each other the real truth of our opinions and intentions. That minute, like right now, as I am writing down these memories, the whole world looked so strange, idiotic, worthy of only one kind of response - bury oneself under rolling pebbles of endless giggling. And what a torture it was - not to dare to laugh!

Feeling that his prestige was disintegrating in the sudden euphoria of the girls, the major abruptly finished our conversation.

CHAPTER 12

Goodness lies within a man's heart for he is happy when he does good and is sad, stupid or mad when he does evil.

George Sand

AFTER ME SEVERAL OF THE GENUINE LUNATICS, FROM WARD #3, were invited to the office, so I was finally convinced that Major Zabusoff had presented me to the medical students as one of the exemplary mental cases. I could be proud of my acting.

That was the good news. The bad news was that Blockhead and Co. recovered from the sulfadiazine and arranged for me and the other newcomer to take the Hospital Oath - a mild version of the Army Oath, so that for striking our asses a slipper instead of belt buckle would be used.

After dinner the sane guys sat down on Blockhead's bed, near the window, talked to each other for a couple of minutes and then announced that the newcomer was getting ten strokes but I, as double-trouble, would get two times more which equaled twenty.

They started with the newcomer, who was a solid muscled fellow turned by his continuous blasting headaches into a mourning crying wimp, a big vulnerable child. Hurting such a poor, defenseless guy would either break one's heart or harden it forever. But at least he didn't have those aminazine lumps, the knots of pain, like me.

Waiting for my turn, I grabbed the bed frame with all my strength and clenched my teeth, breathing anxiously through my nose, so that a long thread of a cobweb hanging from the ceiling started bending and dancing. That dusty string was my only connection with God Almighty, who hinted on every page of the Bible that he created us in his own image.

I didn't know exactly what would happen to me in a couple of minutes, though one thing I knew for sure - I wasn't going to let anybody strip me of my underwear, nobody, unless it be a hot-blooded woman who had a crush on me and got cross-eyed with sudden passion.

Flat, sticky sounds of counted strikes - ...5,6,7... - in the corner of the ward gave me a visual taste of how thick the sole of the slipper, how soft the buttocks, and how close we are to the Stone Age.

"...8,9,10. Good job, fellows, bring in Philosopher."

CHAPTER 13

Ivan the Terrible ordered an elephant to be cut into pieces because he refused to kneel before him.

I WAS APPROACHED BY TWO OF BLOCKHEAD'S BODYGUARDS WHO tore my fingers from the bed frame, dragged me out of bed, hauled me to my feet and twisted my arms, pushing me along the aisle.

My last chance to mess up the execution was to grab the metal arches of the beds on the left and on the right, which I managed to do in one swift lucky moment.

The bodyguards, confused by the impossible task of dragging me and both beds together, stalled and looked at Blockhead for the next order, and the guy on my right, loosened his grip on my wrist.

This fellow had the nose of a lady killer but never mind kill, he couldn't even tackle a woman because he had totally exhausted himself with years of excessive masturbation to the point that he couldn't make it hard anymore. When he realized that his manhood, like a lizard, had lost its extremely useful tail, he tried to hang himself in the company's toilet, was stopped in time by a night guard and, like most suicidal cases, sent here for an examination.

The guy on my left was a collective image of all Russian simpletons: blue lazy eyes, straw hair, thick broad shoulders, minimum spoken words and numerous tattoos with words of wisdom and love confessions - all tangled up in hairy curls and freckles on his chest, arms, legs. Even his eyelids bore a miniature tattoo 'do not awake,' which was readable when he was asleep.

Annoyed with my resistance and the delay of the show, the sane bunch jumped off Blockhead's bed and moved towards me.

I was scared. I was always a coward. But I belong to the breed of attacking cowards. I jerked my right hand, freed it and gave that scarecrow on my left a good, impressive uppercut, technically correct, with a half swing of my upper body.

The guy was frozen, became a wax replica of himself. He motionesslesly looked in front of himself as if he had forgotten and was trying to remember in what slipper he had hidden his cigarette butt.

I wasn't given much time to enjoy my little victory - the big fists arrived, all at once, and threw me into the middle of a kangaroo court. The blows from all directions transformed my honking brain into a speeding fire-engine. I managed to break through the circle into the corridor, ramming somebody's stomach with my head and knocking him over.

The nurse on duty took me straight to her room to paint my bleeding eyebrows with dark brown iodine - 'the color of a grasshopper's saliva', I whispered to myself, because, being possessed by the demon of the poetic hunt, I was always, in every situation, looking for precise or brave comparisons.

CHAPTER 14

Justice without strength is helpless. Strength without justice is tyrannical.

Pascal

THIS SHORT CHAPTER IS DEVOTED TO THE most depressing period in my odd odyssey.

That period lasted 27 days, from the evening of the failed Hospital Oath to the arrival of a private, Oleg Kabakoff, whose wit and friendship saved my life and sanity.

Please remember, that to the 27 days should be added 27 nights, filled with occasional screaming of newcomers or with the blind, transcendental silence of sleepwalkers.

People were coming and going but the games, menu and stink stayed the same. Blockhead left for jail. The punk from Barnaul took over his leadership; his gift of investiture included a pair of old officer's trousers with all four buttons on the fly and a bed in the prestigious corner of the ward, near the window.

Tireless Little Tartar was still demanding for himself two things - justice and a bullet.

Matveev, at age only 19, died in his sleep, of natural causes, or rather from schizophrenia. According to the orderlies' gossip, he had a fast splitting of the brain which led to a fatal brain tumor.

The newcomer with headaches ended up going through sessions of electrotherapy. Twice a week the doctors would put a metal net on his head and run electricity through it. He said to me "You don't feel anything, the very first shock knocks you out unconscious".

Ilyushka Steam-Engine was replaced by a psycho hypochondriac who refused to eat and was fed by force. Once a day a nurse and orderlies would overpower him with their weighty arms and bosoms, tie him to the bed base, stick a plastic funnel in one of his nostrils and pour down a specially cooked, liquid porridge.

Years later, Academic Saharov was fed in exactly the same way. He was a significant contributor to the invention of the nuclear bomb. His honesty and straightforwardness got him a reputation of being mentally disturbed so that when he went on hunger strike in his apartment, to protest human rights violations, he was arrested by the KGB and fed by force. During their barbaric reign the Communists on the one hand starved millions to death at the same time as they were stuffing the throats of dissidents with lumpy gruel - to shut them up.

Belly-Robber got an honorable discharge from the army. After he left I had new neighbors in his spot: the first was Uzbek, who spent a week in the department before the fumes of hashish evaporated from his brain and incredibly wide pupils. Only then he remembered his rape of a woman and was able to stand trial. Our guess was that he wouldn't get less than 10 years of hard labor since the woman was Russian.

After Uzbek arrived Stepan, a dumb, bellowing guy with a bloody bandage on his right hand. He had lost his speech and two fingers in the same evening, while on duty in the regiment kitchen. Chopping firewood for the wood stove, he tried, for fun, to use the ax with different hands in turns and by accident chopped off two fingers on his right hand - the index finger and the middle one - exactly those which provide a discharge from the army.

He was immediately suspected of self-affliction and arrested on the spot. The shock of his arrest, combined with increasing pain, short-circuited the nerves responsible for the vibration of his vocal cords.

I needed a diving mask to ask Stepan questions because, in his desperate attempt to recreate speech, he would sprinkle my face with impatient saliva.

Slava, who was, like me, a poet and a corporal, finally finished his masterpiece.

> The army asylum in Ussuriisk:
> laugh, but you'll be risking death.
> Today it's Gomorrah and it's Sodom tomorrow.
> and always it's sodding Gomorrah.
>
> I didn't take the oath, I yawned instead
> by the banners with all their heraldry
> of carbines and bayonets and soldiery
> and the false smile of the tyrants back from the dead.
>
> The sergeant is epileptic,
> the Lieutenant's a psychopath and has DT's.
> The transcendental Corporal treads his manic path
> yet still a zombie.
>
> I'm that corporal, I sleep and prophesy.
> In the dream of my sleep I remember:
> I walked the knife edge of the subheaven empire,
> rich only in land, open skies everywhere.
> Now I am wedged in here, choking on claustrophobia.

I screamed and recoiled, hating myself and my country,
because of my conscience.

I hadn't slept and now I doze.
As they beat me down with their punishments,
I often dream of a pedestal of bronze,
on which stands the Informer Rampant.

I'm not ill, but I sleep from sunrise to sunset.
In the night, the sodomite Major sings when he's tight
and his four carat tears flow.
The hash-head Uzbek crawls round the floor;
the kleptomaniac steals from himself;
the purple-nosed Private drops his drawers
and plays with his private self.

Seeing - yes, I can see as I sleep
drugged, bottomless, deeper than deep.
The air of the Pacific Ocean I saw
with a jagged-toothed snore.

I can just see those fat martial faces
who'll discharge me or send me off to the military jail.
I'm asleep and have slept
half my life on manuscripts or Ms's.

I'm asleep and I'm blind -
terror stands out on my back like a page of Braille.
I'm asleep and I'm deaf.
Silence hovers - a decapitated bird flails.

The soles of my feet press against the shadows of my friends,
my pulsing temples repel the shadows of the gallows.
Around me is the music of a whirling carousel
but my waking is just before death.

Luckily, my new neighbor on my right was also a quiet guy, a
pious 'idiot'. Sergey, probably the most religious guy in the world. He
would zealously cross himself all day long with the Old Believer's squeeze
of two fingers but because of the speed with which he did it the crosses
looked more like black magic circles, drawn in the air in front of his face. I
never got out of him any explanation of what exactly his faith was and why
he chose such a tiring, unrewarding way of worshipping.

The funny thing about Sergey was that if his eyes looked straight at
heaven and his right hand was more than ever engaged in making crosses,

then I could bet that at the very same moment his other hand was stealing something from the bed cabinet, which we shared between the two of us. That's how my toothpaste, pencil and half a stack of my precious airmail envelopes vanished.

I didn't write letters to anyone and wouldn't have needed the envelopes if they hadn't had a high exchange rate on the asylum's black market. I could easily trade a single envelope with an imprinted stamp for four lumps of sugar or for 10 minutes of back massage or for 24 hour possession of a colorful brochure called 'Operable Breast Cancer and Histologically Involved Auxiliary Lymph Nodes' - the only reading available so far except the loose pages of last year's wall calendar.

Of course I wanted to keep in touch with my friends and relatives but it was a well known fact that all our letters went through censorship in the nurses' room. And if I wrote something special, for the eyes and spectacles of the senior nurse, then folks at home either wouldn't get my letter or would get it and faint in bewilderment. Nobody in my family had the slightest idea where I was. They thought I was still a corporal on active duty, sanding our frosty skies with an abrasive glance in search of American airplanes and other kinds of UFO's. So I only received letters, readdressed by the regiment postmaster, until one morning, at a round, Major Zabusoff marched into my private life with a thoughtful ultimatum.

"Papadin, I have a feeling your parents worry about you not writing to them. Soon it's Mother's Day, 8th of March, let your stepmother or girlfriend know you are still alive. Please, by the end of the week."

In case it was a trap and my letter would be thoroughly analyzed, vivisected like a poor helpless frog, I decided to send just my picture - gloomy me with my stupid corporal's stripes.

I asked a senior nurse to rescue my photo from the bag of my belongings, and wrote on the back of it a short inscription, in the style of the French symbolists.

"Dear Luba, Winter is not over yet but Spring is already on its way. A lot of 220 volt kisses. Yours Valentin."

I was pleased with the message. For Major Zabusoff such inappropriate laconism would be strange enough not to look strange.

And, to slightly snobbish Luba, it would be another comforting reminder of my poetic extravagancy. It would also be very satisfying for me, when I came back home and found this picture on Luba's chest of drawers, to flick my glossy face and say something, triumphant, 'Hello, corporal, hello there, how many cockroaches did your slipper smash to-day?'

After I had sealed the envelope and spat out on the floor the sour taste of glue I sighed with relief: it's done but that's it, no more writing, my madness is strictly spoken. Now I could concentrate more on the main issue: how to survive until the discharge. This was becoming increasingly more difficult because slowly I was beginning to feel that my own sanity was at stake.

The risk of really going mad was more real and dangerous than the knives of the malingerers. In every cell of my brain I felt the pressure of my acting. It was becoming more and more apparent to me that faking madness was the surest way of losing one's marbles. No wonder not many people tried to go this way. And those who tried didn't want to, or rather, were not able to tell their stories. It's something to consider.

Every word I spoke out to impress the doctors and inmates, did not die with the sounds of my voice, but came back to me as an echo and started sprouting in my mind with the powerful force of fast growing weeds, choking my normal concepts, interfering with basic thinking.

The depressing atmosphere of the asylum turned every sound around me into the clanging cymbals of a mass funeral.

I felt like a non-smoker riding in a train compartment for smokers: you slow down your breathing, you even stop breathing for several seconds but it only leads you to a deeper gasp. That's how I was forced to inhale daily, with all my poor mind, the poisonous fumes of others' madness.

CHAPTER 15

Pleasure is often spoiled by describing it.

Stendhal

MY PHYSICAL SHAPE WAS NOT BETTER THAN MY mental one. After the latest beating, my jaws and ribs were very sore and whenever malingerers pushed me or kicked I couldn't stop my tears.

CHAPTER 16

Madness is to think of too many things in succession too fast, or of one thing too exclusively.

Voltaire

I WAS SO TIRED OF PAIN AND THE NERVOUS anticipation of it that gradually I became addicted to the anesthetic effect of total indifference. Now, special thanks to the inmates of Ward #2, I didn't have to pretend to have slurred speech and heavy duty gloominess. They were real.

And the gloomier my look the brighter shined the pleasant endless fantasies behind my fossilized eyeballs. Very often I fantasized about being a ghost - invisible, invulnerable ghost, made of silence and midnight moonlight. I dreamed about the opportunity to die without dying, to walk from life to death, and then from death to second life without painful and bureaucratic procedures such as agony, judgment, penitence and so on.

I was sick and tired of my sensitive body. It seemed to be so wonderful, liberating to escape from the physical form, to dump it like a prickly ugly sweater. I wanted to be just a spirit. This desire, premature at my age, was bringing me closer and closer to the idea of suicide.

Several times, lying on my side and flying in my mind, as usual, from nowhere to nowhere, I scratched my veins with a straightened paper clip - superficially, not deep, not to kill myself yet to stir up thinking about voluntary death. I hated the idea of going to another world without having a go with a woman.

To me death could offer me everything I wanted except erotic satisfaction. I decided to wait for a discharge and use the paper-clip for cleaning my finger-nails. I couldn't possibly die and leave some stranger's hands in charge of Luba's breasts. No way. It wasn't only that I remembered Luba, she also remembered me. Almost every night, long after I swallowed aminazine, her beaming big blue eyes were sliding, like moon light, down the frosty window in search of my forsaken soul. Once her eyes were so bright, they woke up the inmates on my side of the ward, who grumbled, in their typical stupidity, that the drunken driver of an ambulance forgot to turn off his lights.

Still, the main self-afflicted depression, like an oversized winter hat, was closing the view around me. Somewhere, outside these greasy cold walls, there were rational conversations, decency, music, fresh air and sunlight, delightful luxuries of a half forgotten past. I wanted all these so much that, in a paradoxical state of superstition, didn't dare to believe I could have them. I didn't believe that I could ever return to normal life among normal people.

This was bad. I knew what was happening, but I seemed unable to prevent myself from sinking imperceptibly into a mental quagmire.

CHAPTER 17

Who can feel sure that he has ever been understood? We all die unknown.
Honore de Balzac

TO WHOMEVER WAS WATCHING OVER ME FROM THE seventh sky, guardian angels or a higher authority with wider wings, the sight must have been pathetic. That's why, ten days before my official discharge and shortly before my going totally cuckoo, an uncommon, smiling soldier, Oleg Kabakoff, walked into Bedlam.

He was met at the doors by the traditional Welcoming Committee - the noisy jumping zoo in turbans. But their eagerness to frighten him got smashed to smithereens against his friendly smile.

> I never saw a man who looked
> > With such a wistful eye
> Upon that little tent of blue
> > Which prisoners call the sky,
> And at every drifting cloud that went
> > With sails of silver by.

I jealously spotted the shine of a superior intelligence on the slope of the newcomer's forehead. He was too positive, relaxed, polite to be a criminal. Neither was he surrounded by those nagging enervating vibrations, which accompany a mosquito's flight or a human's hidden madness.

> I walked, with other souls in pain,
> > Within another ring,
> And was wondering if the man had done
> > A great or little thing...

Kabakoff was put into Ward #1, but very soon, because of his sociable character and his beautiful, strikingly musical renditions of Dave Brubeck variations ('Take Five' and others) he was heard and welcome in different corners of the department.

It was the first lesson he taught me: people here were not as bad as I perceived them. I myself was partly responsible for my mistreatment in the hospital. My well acted paranoia didn't have much to do with it. I was disliked simply because I didn't like anybody. My cherished unwillingness to compromise my moral principles for an immoral government had fossilized into an annoying monument of pride. And a prideful man is like an empty tuna fish can on the side-walk: everybody, including God Almighty, wants to kick it. I got what I asked for.

The second lesson I learned from Oleg was: I could have got a discharge much more easily, without damaging my mind with self-inflicted madness. It would have been enough to stage a suicide attempt. Officers are scared of soldiers who try to kill themselves. They send them straight to psychiatrists and refuse to take them back, because in the barracks the suicidal types never quit their search for a hanging rope and sometimes their contempt for life is wide enough to include shooting at whoever else is available - the nearest platoon mates or commanders. It was a vulnerable spot in the army structure; Oleg realized it and without hesitation used it for his advantage. He was brought here for observation, after a 'failed suicide attempt'.

Before the army Oleg had studied math and physics for three years at the University of Irkutsk until his expulsion for 'immoral behavior, unworthy of a Soviet student'. This term referred to his two favorite activities - complaining about the pollution of Lake Baikal, the deepest lake in the world, and playing the saxophone in an evening restaurant. In the late 60's jazz was called 'the burp of bourgeois decadence' and was illegal in many cities.

As soon as the university expelled Oleg, the army called him up. At his military base Oleg staged a skillful suicide attempt. He took off his boots and put the barrel of his Kalashnikov under his chin and his big toe on the trigger. At this point his fellow soldiers grabbed him and took the gun away - which was what he had intended to happen.

Oleg didn't use the word 'staged', but I could read between the lines of his story. He also saw through me and, in return, didn't ask provocative questions about my 'philosophy.'

We left the delicate subject of madness soaking in silence until better, safer times when we would both be free, in loose civvies, bragging without fear of being heard.

> Like two doomed ships that pass in storm
> > We had crossed each other's way:
> We made no sign,we said no word,
> > We had no word to say;
> For we did not meet in the holy night,
> > But in the shameful day.
>
> A prison wall was round us both,
> > Two outcast men we were:
> The world had thrust us from its heart,

And God from out His care:
And the iron gin that waits for Sin
Had caught us in its snare.

★★★

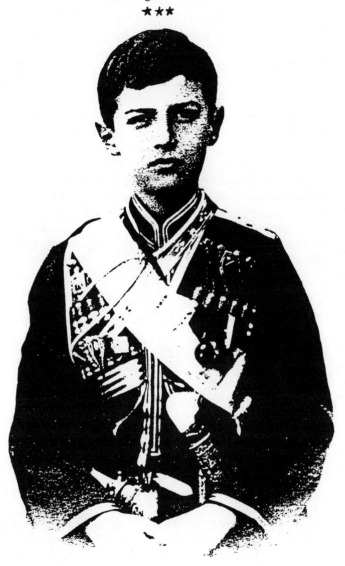

Alyosha in one of my dreams

CHAPTER 18

A learned man is not learned in all things; but an able man is able in all, even in ignorance.

Montaigne

I DID MY BEST TO BECOME OLEG'S CLOSE FRIEND. It was absolutely necessary for staying sane, and pleasant for my Ego. We often played chess with chess pieces made of chewed white and black bread - there was no need to paint them! One day we had real fun contriving a model to represent the psychology of Soviet man...

If you take a strip of paper and glue the ends together, you have a ring. One side, the inner side, symbolizes the sphere of insane thoughts. The outer side represents the normal, logical side of the mind's activity. A ring like that is the model of normal psychology. Anyone can see that the outside is the outside and the inside is the inside: sanity and insanity in their normal relationship to each other. There is a clear boundary between them, the edge of the paper.

But the model of Soviet man's psychology is the Mobius strip, a ring of paper twisted once. It has only one side.

A fly, or if you wish a man's thought, crawling along the Mobius strip would cover the whole ring and return to its starting point without once crossing the edge of the paper, and yet its journey would have taken it through the outer and inner sides of the ring, the light side and dark side, the sane side and the mad side, without any distinction being made between them.

For each Soviet citizen, propaganda has twisted the paper strip of his mind far back in childhood, in the kindergartens where the best toy was given to the loudest little singer of the state hymn or to the seven year-old boy who reported his politically immature parents to the police. The paper strip is stealthily twisted one time by the power of the state, and distinctions between true and false, good and evil, sane and insane, become deeply, almost irrevocably blurred.

When I say 'Soviet' I refer not only to my impoverished, bitter, malnutritioned compatriots, led astray by twentieth century lies. According to the latest journeys of my Third Telepathic Eye through Past and Future, Soviet marching troops have polluted every hour in mankind's history.

The Soviets sat still in the wooden horse and then, at night, stormed and destroyed Troy. The Soviets crucified Christ, nailed him to the cross made of Siberian Douglas fir. Flattened and burned Jerusalem. Burned the militant virgin, Joan of Arc, at the stake. Bewitched themselves, they led witch hunts with the burning torches of the Holy Inquisition and barbecued half of the bravest part of medieval Europe.

Put Galileo Galilei on his knees. Beheaded Thomas Moore. Pierced the innocence of native Americans with Toledo steel. Sent Dostoevsky to labor camp. Shot Abraham Lincoln.

They sunk the 'Lusitania'. Printed 'Mein Kampf'. Bombed Kiev, Leningrad, Dresden. Made Stalin generallisimo.

Injected, during medical experiments, horse blood into pregnant Chinese women and, as a mercy, chopped them up with noble Samurai swords.

Shot down a South- Korean airliner. Tried to overthrow Gorbachev. Refused to give me an advance for writing this book and threatened to cut off the phone and electricity line in my Californian house because as a sign painter I hardly break even for a family of seven.

Oleg and I made many of these paper Mobius strips and wore them on our wrists like bracelets. To the medical staff it was just further proof of our incurable madness.

CHAPTER 19

All human misery comes only from this: that we are incapable of remaining quietly in our rooms

Pascal

ONE DAY, WHEN OLEG AND I WERE CHATTING ON A bench in the corridor, the punk from Barnaul with his new bodyguard, Boris, decided that they would teach us a lesson about who was who.

"Look around, Boris, look what we have to put up with every day..."

"Everyone's smoking... but nobody offers a cigarette. Isn't it the pits?.. And what's all this hanging junk?" - Punk gestured towards our Mobius strips and bent down towards the unsuspecting Oleg.

If I had hesitated another second relaxed Oleg would have been knocked out. I stood up in a flash. Then, much to the surprise of the inmates and to my own unbelief, bombarded Punk's face with a series of what we call in Siberia 'village' punches - punches from the left and right, aimed at the jaw, without much technique but with a lot of fury.

I didn't care much about the consequences. My hatred had shrunk my fear. That minute I had one purpose in life - to make Punk's face look like a red lamp shade around a 100 watt bulb.

My knuckles crashing into the enemy's teeth gave me sweet, high voltage shocks of pure satisfaction. Punk was nailed to the wall without a chance to counterattack. Finally Boris and some orderlies moved in between us and separated us, disconnecting the wires of my anger.

I thought I would get a shot of sulfadiazine for the fit of rage. I didn't. I thought the thugs would beat me to death that very night but obviously they needed more time to come up with a special menu for revenge...They badly miscalculated because the next morning Major Zabusoff invited me to his office where two guys with blue shoulder loops were standing looking attentively at me. "You are going home, Papadin. Here is your escort - Sergeant Marruk and Private Shevaldeshev. Get back to the ward, bring your personal belongings. They'll wait."

The orderly took me back to the ward. I gave my soap, toothpaste, envelopes and a big hug to my dear friend Oleg. We exchanged addresses.

I never saw sad men who looked
With such a wistful eye

> Upon that little tent of blue
>   We prisoners called the sky,
> And at every happy cloud that passed
>   In happy freedom by.

Before the imbeciles realized that I was leaving Bedlam for good, unpunished, I teasingly waved good-by to them and to my crumpled blanket which lay on my bed - like the empty cocoon of my deserted past. I followed the orderly through the main door to the tiny storage room where my belongings were.

My bundled up overcoat stank of mice and mildew but for my soul, this was the smell of freedom's threshold.

Part III

WAKING BEFORE DEATH

CHAPTER 1

We get so much in the habit of wearing disguises before others that we finally appear disguised before ourselves.

Francois, Duke de La Rochefoucauld

A WEEK LATER I WAS BACK IN THE URALS, in Magnitogorsk. I was nearly home. Not quite home, though, because, according to the bureaucratic procedure, to soften up my transfer to civilian life, I was put in a civilian asylum, which was a vast improvement. Compared to the military hospital it was like a rest-home for retired ballerinas. There were visiting hours practically every day. As I had hoped in my pounding heart and simultaneously pulsing balls, the first visitor was my deeply puzzled girlfriend Luba.

She was waiting in the visiting room looking sunburnt and rather uncomfortable in a tight-fitting white T-shirt. Her shopping bag full of tasty goodies and her very feminine profile were everything I dreamed to touch. At the sight of me shuffling into the room Luba tried to cover her confusion by winking conspiratorially

It scared me a bit that Luba might smear the still fresh colors of my self-portrait as a madman. But this was one of the old fears which I now had to get rid of, and so I proudly told her: "You see I've come back even sooner than you and I dared to hope."

Even after Luba went home I was happy. How could I complain? Of white walls in the ward, beds with chrome bedheads, starched pillow-cases, small herds of peaceful lunatics, the spring sunshine coming through the clean broad window, no limit on white bread in the mess hall, TV each evening for an hour or more if it's an international hockey game, what more could I wish for after the dungeons of the Ussuriisk hospital?

I was sleeping; sleeping without fear of being beaten, humiliated or exposed. For the first week I enjoyed the relative safety of the civilian hospital. This security was confirmed when I glanced at my medical history as it lay on the psychiatrist's desk during my first interview with her. The up side down capital letters of the diagnosis declared : "Schizophrenia, paranoid form, manic depressive type."

A day later, when my father was given a copy of my History of Illness, Luba brought it into the visiting room and we triumphantly savored every word.

NOTARIZED COPY

HISTORY OF ILLNESS #130116

2 April 1970, The Military Medical Commission of Military
Base # 86730, located on the premises of Military Base
86730 in Ussuriisk, concluded:

1. Last name, first name, middle name : Papadin, Valentin
Grigory

2. Rank: Corporal

3. Military base: # 62546, Spassk-Dalniy

4. Date of birth: 1951.

5. Entered service in Soviet Army and Navy: November 1969.

6. Enlisting Military Committee: West Coast District Military
Committee of the City of Magnitogorsk, Chelyabinsk Region.

7. Membership: Member of Young Communist League.

8. Civilian profession: none.

9. Height:174 cm, weight: 62 kg, circumference of the chest:
93 cm.

10. Complaints: none.

11. Brief analysis: patient does not consider himself to be sick.
Report from the Military Base contains following facts: as of
January 1970 patient showed distracted reaction, forgetfulness,
as a team leader stopped being demanding towards his
subordinates, behaved in noticeably strange manner.

12. Has been going through period of observation and medical
treatment since.

13. Given medical treatment: Aminazine.

14. Results of objective check up and observation: correct
constitution of the body. Pathology of the internal organs is
absent. Brain and scalp nerves are adequate. Skin reflexes are
steady, alive. Pathological reflexes, disturbed emotions,
discoordination of movements are not found. Perception is
pathologically changed. Patient insists that he can feel from a
long distance what's going on far away from him.

"They think and I feel their thoughts". Expresses his 'own opinions' in philosophical questions. Makes such statements as: " Since I have new ideas I should go to the Theological Seminary in Kiev. My point of view is contrary to popular established doctrines. I have ideas which are challenging to the main stream of thinking." Spends days in writing 'theses', not being interested in anything else. Patient doesn't seem to be oppressed by his confinement to the department.

Doesn't criticize the political establishment.

Blood samples:.................................No sugar in blood.

15. Diagnosis: Schizophrenia, paranoid form.

16. Conclusion of the Commission:

a. Corporal Valentin Papadin is considered to be unfit for performing his military duty. Dismissed from the ranks and enlistment. Action taken is based on Chapter 4-b of the Special Medical Attachment to the Order of the Ministry of Defense, dated September 21, 1966.

b. Sickness developed during active military service.

17. Needs an escort.

Chairman of the Commission Colonel...../Signature/

The conclusion of the Commission is confirmed and recorded on the 13th day of April 1970.

My main mission was over. I had passed all stations on the way, speeding like an express train, and now I had to stop or at least slow down, to avoid a head-on collision with real madness. There was no need to continue. I had reached that point in psychiatric diagnostics beyond which no doctor dares to doubt or reconsider.

The reason lies not in the solidarity of the doctors who don't like to contradict or undermine each other but in the nature of psychiatry itself, where once you have shown the symptom of madness you are already classified.

It reminded me of the state's attitude to its citizens: once you have been noticed to stray from the majority, you are indelibly labeled as an enemy of the whole nation, as a danger to state security.

I had reached the point beyond which the louder you shout "I am wise", the more concerned doctors become. Now it was time to behave properly. No more philosophizing or more black moods, no more zombiness, no more sophisticated dialogs with my own shadow. From now on I was all right. Because I was.

One day passed, two, three, a week, second week - there was no effect, no reaction from the medical staff... My miraculous rapid 'recovery' went unnoticed exactly the way some time ago my 'madness' did not strike the platoon mates. Bummer! Now I had turned the record over but nobody wanted to listen to it. At my next interview with the chief psychiatrist, an old, wrinkled, partially blind woman, I told her that the air of my homeland had helped me to get rid of all noisy illusions about my achievements in philosophy.

"I am so happy for you, Valentin, so happy."

A tear in the eye of that sentimental granny was enlarged by the thick lenses of her glasses to the size of a ten gallon fish tank, full of wriggling red octopuses, or burst blood vessels to be precise.

"But tell me, Valentin, did you really believe that you were the cleverest being in the universe?"

"Oh yes, of course I *did.*"

The past tense was passionately emphasized.

The lady smiled benignly at the senior nurse, then, stroking an expensive Siamese cat sitting on her lap, loudly announced his unusual name - 'Insulin, Insulin.'

That evening I called home from the hospital booth. "Hi, Dad, I guess I'll see you tomorrow. Could you take a day off to keep me company? I'd appreciate it."

Next morning I was awakened early by the jingling of a steel trolley bearing sterilized syringes. The sleepy nurse who was pushing it explained to me confidentially that a course of a newly discovered drug 'Insulin' worked wonders in cases like mine.

It was a thunderclap from a clear sky. I couldn't believe my ears. I felt like tearing them off for catching such a dreadful message. I thought I was a smart cookie, outwitting everybody, but, in fact, I was the dumbest fool who had ever trapped himself in the deadly labyrinths of the psychiatric system.

Even while I was basking in the certitude of my proximate release, a new danger was casting its shadow over me. There was a rumor circulating among the alcoholics in this shiny, clean, civilian asylum that younger mental patients (my age!), in good physical health (me again!), and without close relatives (what if my father dies?), WERE BEING USED AS ORGAN DONORS...

The rumor had it that dead lunatics of 15 years and older were buried with missing eyes and suspiciously hollow spaces under rough stitches in the area of heart, liver and kidneys. I imagined myself lying without my eyes on the icy cement of the mortuary and howled in hysterics. The nurse rushed to get help and a mug of water.

My feeling of desperation was very acute, but my howling was cut short by a friendly voice from the depth of my mind: "To hell with all this mediocrity, they are not worth your worry. Who cares about this life, anyway? You are great, you are immortal! Ignore the idea that a crafty sergeant will poke out your eyes and sell them to the blind leaders of the blind, to the nursing home called Soviet Politburo - your eyes will be restored and blue again on the front page of every European encyclopedia. Just think - on the FRONT page!"

In terror I recognized that insidious voice which I had heard on the train from Ussuriisk. And I knew what the existence of this voice really was - a slide into schizophrenia...

Since the train journey this voice had become louder and more logical. It had demonstrated a good knowledge of my character, paralyzing my self-criticism and feeding my sense of superiority. It meant I had betrayed myself and was splitting slowly in two.

I was not only surrounded by powerful enemies - a gang of experienced psychiatrists - but I myself was the leading protagonist in the treason against myself.

CHAPTER 2

No man is exempt from saying silly things. The misfortune is to say them seriously.

Montaigne

THE INSULIN TREATMENT LASTED TWO MONTHS. DURING THE first ten days the dose of insulin, injected in both arms, was increased until I fell unconscious and shook with convulsions. These were treated by tying me to the bed with two sheets. After regaining consciousness I had to drink a thick sugary syrup to compensate for the artificially created lack of glucose in my blood. This 'up-to-date treatment' was introduced after doctors noticed that people with diabetes had convulsions after excessive doses of insulin.

The logic of Soviet psychiatry was very simple: if a broken radio sometimes starts working again after being shaken or even deliberately dropped on the floor, there may also be a chance that a human's mind can get back to normal logic after a good 'twist-and-shake' arranged by insulin injections.

During treatment my face had became fat and bloated and I saw the heroic image of me, reflected in Luba's eyes, gradually shrinking.

I spent my birthday, June 15, observing the convulsions of others. My treatment was over but the sore bruises on my wrists and ankles, the pale full moon of my face and that impudent voice were just the prelude to my future requiem...

Because I was going to be buried alive, there was no chance to get out of that hospital officially. The only way was to escape. I looked at Luba with eyes narrowed by my swollen cheeks.

"I want to get out of here. In your clothes. Before the bastards grind my bones."

She regarded me doubtfully. "Let's wait until the autumn. I'll help you, but not in your condition. Wake up from the insulin first."

As it turned out I was lucky again. The chief psychiatrist left on holiday which for people of her profession are as long as for miners - the whole summer. Her assistant, an intelligent young woman, took her place. She interviewed me with a super modern touch - a tape recorder playing religious Handel, in an unspeakable foreign language, either German or English cockney.

85

"Valentin, You never asked for a note-book to write down your ideas."

"Who said I needed it? I hate philosophy. I never had any ideas. Oh maybe I had but they are gone. Gone. Long time ago. Five centuries ago."

"I thought..."

"No, you are wrong. I hate note-books. All I want is reheated spaghetti with meatballs in the cafe opposite my house."

"You might be right, Spinoza, maybe the domestic environment will help you more than insulin. We could give you a try for a month or two... What do you think?"

I wasn't sure in the interview whether she was teasing or trying to provoke me. But in two days I was at home. God bless her heart and long hairy legs.

CHAPTER 3

The more you say, the less people remember. The fewer the words, the greater the profit.

Fenelon

I HAD PLENTY OF GIGGLES WITH LUBA AND MY FRIENDS about my adventures in the freezing catacombs of the army asylum. I was a kind of hero. Telling my stories, I enjoyed imitating regiment officers, platoon mates, nurses, doctors, making them look stupid and ignorant - an easy tempting thing to do when you feel safe and are talking to your old friends, opening a second or even third bottle of cheap Bulgarian cognac.

I also told them about Oleg, how helpful his friendship was.

"Have you written him?"

"Sent a postcard to Irkutsk, at his home. He must have been discharged by now."

"He sounds likes a neat guy with a lot to say."

CHAPTER 4

Dying is the greatest task we have to do but practice can give us no assistance.

Montaigne

MY BUDDIES WERE RIGHT: OLEG HAD A LOT TO SAY - more than I ever expected or wanted to hear. That's why only now, many years later, I feel confident enough to share the context of his letter.

'Hello, Valentin, hello!

Thank you for your cheerful card. I laughed reading how you tried to get free rides on city buses showing the drivers your self-issued Certificate of Insanity.

Still, my friend, your happy spirit didn't change my decision to move into another world. I am talking about death, not emigration...

After Ussuriisk I was more fortunate than you - spent only two weeks in the civilian asylum and got back to my mum and jazz-band.

But life in a 'sane' community immediately shocked me, totally demoralized me. I forgot how many people lie for money, career, security. What a horrible sight: even the deaf and dumb, begging for change on street corners, learn how to lie in sign language, drawing lies with their lips and fingers, so that even silence became a deceiving falsetto. Everything has been twisted - words, silence, music.

I can't take it any more. I am escaping from this life through a trivial loop-hole, called a hanging rope...'

And I couldn't continue reading without a gasp of fresh air. I took the letter to the balcony.

> 'It is sweet to dance to violins
>> When Love and Life are fair:
> To dance to flutes, to dance to lutes,
>> Is delicate and rare:
> But it is not sweet with nimble feet
>> To dance upon the air'.

Oleg, Oleg, I never would have thought...

'By the time you receive my letter I will already be nicely dressed, shaved and buried. What you are reading right now is in fact my self-epitaph.

I am talking to you from from a seven foot depth...

88

(Do you know why in Russia the graves are seven feet deep? It's the maximum height of a man, it insures that when by any chance a dead man rises to cause troubles he is still in the ground; he moves, walks through the thickness of the soil but he can't get out to the air on the surface, and the maximum damage he does with the top of his head are the zig-zags of trenches and ridges on the lawn which we think are the work of moles.)

And, finally, the main subject of the letter - YOU and... ALYOSHA.

We chatted a lot together, didn't we?- on all benches in the corridor, and very often you mentioned that twelve year old kid, a strange non-talking personality, who you claimed to have seen at least three times in three different places - on the train, in Spassk-Dalniy and in Ussuriisk.

Listening to you I was intrigued and puzzled:

a. How could it be possible that neither sergeants nor recruits spotted Alyosha during that very long train journey with endless inspections, sweepings, tidyings?

b. What a strange non-healing scratch he had !

c. If Alyosha never said to you a single word, how did you know his name?

d. Why were his clothes either expensive antiques or totally out of season?

To be honest, Alyosha in all your stories looked to me like a product of your imagination.

But I had to prove it.

And I wasn't able to do that until one day I put together two things - the time you first noticed the boy in the train compartment and the name of the station which the train was passing at that very moment.

According to your recollection of those events, Alyosha walked out of the dusk of the compartment when the train was crossing the city limit of Sverdlovsck.

The name 'Sverdlovsck' wouldn't have said much to me if I didn't know the old name of the city - Yekaterinburg - a solemn place where in 1918 the Bolsheviks murdered Tsar Nikolai and his whole family, Alyosha and his sisters.

All of them were shot at close range, defaced with strong acids, dumped in an old mine and burned. Knowing that you also knew about the massacre I could easily figure out what associations stormed your restless mind....

And here is my explanation of the 'Alyosha phenomenon.' When the train passed the station's sign, lit at night, your feelings of despair and frustration, caused by the inevitable military service, joined another tragic flock - the thoughts and associations connected with the royal family, who tried to stop the flying bullets with hands and screaming.

Among those killed, Tsarevitch Alyosha (shot in the face), being a male and only three years younger, related to you most. That's why from that very night you subconsciously identified yourself with the tsarevitch. Then you, or rather your subconscious, took the next step - you projected Alyosha's image in the air from photos of him you had memorized in the past as you went through pre-revolutionary magazines. Finally this image was made alive by your feeling of aloneness, which is, in my opinion, the most creative power in the universe.

The children of Tsar Nikolai II

Perhaps, the word 'alive' doesn't quite express the quality of your hallucinations but, you must agree, it describes them pretty well.

Let's look at the encyclopedia:

"The symptoms of mental disorders are many and varied, but the following are among the most frequently encountered. Illusions are misinterpretations of existing ideas or phenomena, which the patient refers to himself. Delusions are imagined but fixed ideas of persecution, jealousy, grandeur, illness, or sin, based on simple coincidence. Hallucinations are perceptions of sights, sounds, or odors which do not really exist, although they are very real to the patient."

What do you think?

Don't get defensive, old fruit-cake, look at the pictures I am sending and decide for yourself whether everything I said is correct.

I just don't want you to have illusions about the dark corners of your mentality.

Hey, Valentin, look at these pictures.

Doesn't "the train boy" look like a part of this royal family? And share the same Cossack style uniform as Tsar of Russia Nikolai II?

I am planning my suicide for 7 p.m. - a border hour, underlined with red by the horizon. 45 minutes left. My closeness to death should convince you of the sincerity of this letter.

Good bye.
Your short-time buddy Oleg Kabakoff.
August 14, 1970.
6.15 p.m..'

CHAPTER 5

Marriage is the only adventure open to the cowardly.

Voltaire

FOR ME OLEG'S LETTER HAD THE SAME STRANGLING effect on me as the rope he had used for hanging himself. It contained a true revelation about my hallucinatory perception of reality. It was cruel evidence that I had gone mad before I started acting.

Whether to be grateful to Oleg for telling the truth or to hate him for leaving me in confusion, I didn't know. Meanwhile I dropped several comforting lines in a postcard to his mother. Poor woman, probably wouldn't last long after such a loss. I also told her about the coming wedding with Luba and formally invited her.

Another question for me was my girlfriend. 'Should I tell her about this new twist in my mental history? Maybe I should. To give her an example of marital honesty right before our wedding.'

Luba's reaction was encouraging.

"Hey, Valentin, you are taking me as is, and vice versa. You are nutty and I wear spectacles - so we're even."

"Are you sure?"

"Positive."

"Luba, you are wonderful. I forgive you my undeserved virginity."

At the wedding reception, the suburban house of Luba's parents couldn't hold all the invited guests. Our friends and relatives were chatting outside, passing opened bottles around.

It was a bit chilly, and, being in a hurry to warm up, many men got drunk fast. Their happy burping and risque joking moved out of the yard into the nearby street, under the feet of determinedly depressed pedestrians.

My short and stout uncle Grisha acted as an accordionist. It was not easy to recognize the folksongs he was playing. Amateur musician that he was, he kept his chin on the edge of the keyboard in order to watch his rugged uncertain fingers and had the serious, self-absorbed expression of a little boy who has climbed onto the neighbors' fence to spy on busy adults. Soon, fortunately for Apollos, god of fine art and music, and unfortunately for our fun-thirsty guests, uncle lost his balance after vodka, tripped over the bumper of a just arrived taxi, and, being strapped to the accordion with wide leather belts, fell down right on the accordion which squeaked like an old chair and let out a sigh from its punctured bellows.

Confused and sorrowful, uncle started announcing his verdict of not-guilty while lying on the ground. "I knew I would have a bad day today: this morning my wife broke a mirror. I said to her, 'Broken mirrors bring bad luck, get rid of it, dump it in a garbage can.' So guess what she did? Glued the pieces together and put the mirror right back on the table. Stubborn old cow. Look what she's done! Look at this mess. What will we do without music?"

"Don't worry, Uncle Grisha (I helped him get up) "I'll find a guitar or something else."

"How about my sax? It might come in handy." (A newly arrived guest slammed the trunk of a taxi and lifted out a saxophone case with an airport tag tied to the handle.)

His familiar voice was tightly interwoven with a familiar smile. It could only be Oleg. And that's exactly who it was. He

> ...walked the yard
> In the suit of shabby gray:
> His cricket cap was on his head,
> And his step seemed light and gay,
> But I never saw a man who looked
> So wistfully at the day.

"Hello, old fruit cake, congratulations! You married too young! Still, it's better than getting addicted to moonshine or joining the Communist Party."

"Oleg, is it really you?"

"In person. Flew for twelve hours to participate in the happy event."

"I am so glad you didn't do that...that..."

"Hadn't a chance...I was taking the letter to the mailbox across the street when suddenly I smelled smoke: the neighbor's cottage had caught fire from a welding torch held by a roofer who was working on the gutters. I knew that inside the house there were toddlers - twins - and their nutty grandma with dozens of cats, singing birds and parrots. The blaze was furious, the siren of the fire engine was blocks away and the grandma in panic lost the rest of her mind: she was bringing to the door, one by one, huge cages with hysterical parrots, but completely ignored the screaming in the double-cradle...To make a long story short the kids are fine, the old woman too, and I've been confined to local publicity and hospital treatments: heroic bruises, second degree burns, permanent damage to lungs by smoke inhalation, broken shoulder.. I am prescribed strong painkillers but I'm not taking them."

"Maybe you should."

"No way! Between the two of us, the pain distracts me, kills my suicidal thoughts, hunts them down and devours them, yummmmy. It makes me mentally healthier. My pain reminds me of ferocious wolves which clean the forests of weak and sick deer. Long life to the Wolf of Pain! And to this Silver Beast. Shall I play here or go inside?"

"Here, but ... you said your lungs are hurting.."

"Don't worry, the more it hurts, the better it feels, that's what Mother Russia is all about. Here's the bride. Luba? Nice to meet you, Luba. I brought you a wedding present: 'Take Five', live solo, jet-lag variation."

The guests' younger kids , intrigued by the awkwardly shaped musical instrument, surrounded Oleg.

Luba listened to the chaotic geometry of jazz, hugging me with one arm, rubbing into my borrowed suit the constant rustling of her flashy white wedding dress.

Then she did exactly what she had to as a bride according to the good old Siberian custom which assumes that every husband sooner or later will start beating his wife on a weekly basis. She cried.

But Oleg, engulfed in music, attributed her prophetic tears to the charm of invisible Dave Brubeck. He winked at Luba and bent down, like a hunchback, in a new swing of the tune. The shiny saxophone with numerous little metal loops, nuts, holes, rivets, frighteningly resembled a well oiled antique musket whose barrel Oleg had stuck in his mouth and whose trigger he was now trying to press.

I wish he could see himself through my Third Telepathic Eye.

The noise of a departing taxi gave a delicate shake to my brain and I suddenly remembered something important I had wanted to ask my friend. It was so urgent that I dared to interrupt his music.

"Oleg, do pardon me...Am I continuing to hallucinate or what, but it seems that there were two passengers in the car - you and a teenager of Alyosha's age. Was it really him?"

"I knew you would ask that question. All right, listen, it's not so simple..."

CHAPTER 6

The secret of being a bore is to tell everything.

Voltaire

APOLOGY FROM THE AUTHOR

Don't worry, my friends, I'm not going to leave you in the mist, but I needed time to take a deep breath...

CHAPTER 7

God made repentance the virtue of mankind.

Voltaire

What Oleg said to me next was so piercing that I couldn't tell if he was shouting or whispering.

"... The point, Valentin, is I discovered recently that Alyosha appeared to many and I don't think it's an illusion. It's the conscience of Russia finally awakening. So it's a good sign, don't worry, you don't need a shrink. But probably all we can do is to cry out to God for mercy, asking Him to forgive us, each of us in his own quiet corner."

QUOTED AUTHORS
Poems of Oscar Wilde (Ballad of Reading Gaol) and Valentin
Papadin.

About the author...

Valentin Papadin was born in 1951 in Russia. As a typical Siberian boy he started fist-fighting and writing poetry at an early age.

In 1969, being drafted into the Soviet Air Force, he took on the Soviet system by faking madness in order to get a discharge.

From 1970-1975 he worked as a sign painter in Leningrad (now St. Petersburg). Polishing floors in the daytime, he attended Pedagogical Institute where he studied Russian Language and Literature for four years. His anti-government poems and risky openness in conversations brought him under the close surveillance and harassment of the KGB.

In 1980, after a hunger strike, Valentin was allowed to join his American wife and newborn son in Great Britain. There he worked as a gardener and part-time lecturer. In 1983 he moved to Italy to teach Russian at a FIAT car factory.

At that time his poems and cartoons were published in the leading Russian emigre press in Paris.

Since 1986 he has lived in the U.S.A. A former language instructor in the US Army Defense Language Institute, he now owns a sign company in Northern California.

He lives with his wife and five children near the coast of the Pacific Ocean which separates him from that part of the Soviet peninsula where the events of this book take place.